Get Back in Front

Get Back in Front

45 Precise Rules
for Raises, Promotions and Projects

Brad Cormier

On-Demand Publishing LLC

Copyright © 2014 Bradley R. Cormier

All rights reserved. No Part of this book may be reproduced or utilized in any form or by any means, without permission in writing from the author, except for brief quotations in review articles.

ISBN: 978-1494361730
ISBN-13: 1494361736

This book is dedicated to my children Heather, Emma, Connor, Aidan, Jack and Kathleen.

CONTENTS

ACKNOWLEGEMENTS... i

1 IMAGE IS CRITICAL... 1

2 RESPOND IMMEDIATELY.. 9

    Respond Instantly.. 9

    High Availability.. 11

    Stop What You Are Doing....................................... 12

    Instant, Phone, and Email Messages....................... 13

    Accuracy... 15

3 FINDING AND SELLING ENERGY............................... 17

    Just Get to the Gym... 19

    Reflect Energy... 22

    Find Your Horizon Line.. 24

4 THE IMAGE OF TRACTION... 27

    Advertise Traction... 30

    Motivate Someone.. 32

    Manage Your Boss.. 36

    Long Pole in the Tent... 38

5 MASTER BUREAUCRACY.. 43

6 LEADERSHIP... 47

7	**FIRE DRILLS**..	53
8	**THE MEETING IS YOUR FRANCHISE**.......................	59
	Weekly Leadership Meeting..	60
	Be a Smart Attendee...	67
9	**EXPERT ESTIMATING**...	69
	Top Down Estimating..	71
	Single Best Risk Reducer...	74
	Estimating Format..	76
	Bottom Up Estimating..	79
	Large Project Estimating..	80
	Anchoring..	84
10	**MANAGING REQUIREMENTS**......................................	89
	Never Volunteer Requirements.................................	92
	Saving a Project...	95
11	**PROJECT PLANNING SIMPLIFIED**............................	99
	Gantt Charts...	103
12	**EVERYONE'S A PROJECT MANAGER**.......................	107
	Weakest Link..	108
	Building Accountability..	109
	Make Time for Politics...	110
13	**THE POLITICS OF OFFSHORING**..............................	111

	India..	113
	Visiting India..	117
14	**ONE TEAM OFFSHORING**..	121
	Evolution..	126
	Next Big Step..	129
15	**MANAGING REMOTE STAFF**......................................	133
16	**FASTER CAREER ADVANCEMENT**............................	139
	My Experience..	142
	APPENDIX..	145

ACKNOWLEDGMENTS

Thanks to my wife Amy for her lifetime support and for modeling the lead on the front cover.

Thanks to my editor O.M.

Thanks to Eric Kelly Photographie at (www.erickellyphoto.com).

Thanks to my technology teams in Cleveland, Pittsburgh, Nashville, and Pune for amazing results every time.

Thanks to all my friends and family that helped bring this project together.

1

IMAGE IS CRITICAL

Many years ago, I was introduced to a concept that shocked me at a training session in my company. Each person's career success can be broken down into varying degrees of image and performance. The theory was that your career growth is based on these elements at these percentages.

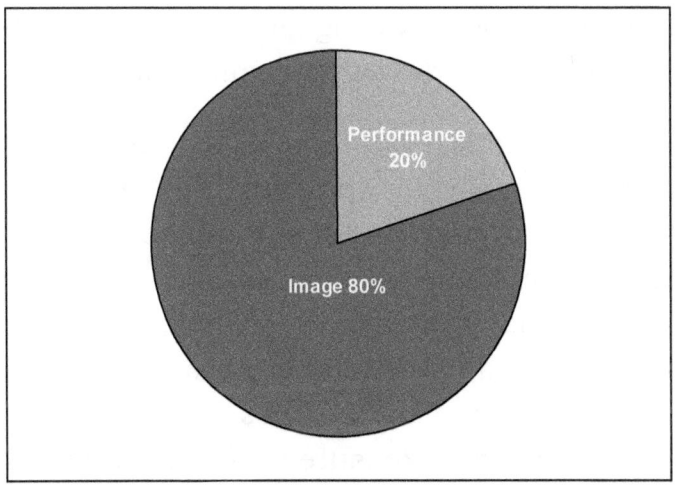

Performance: This is the measurement of how well you produce day-to-day work, meet milestones, reach financial goals, and supply quality with your work.

Image: It is how others perceive the performance of your work and your ability to impress others.

At that time, I was a senior project manager working for a top ten bank. I considered myself to be a very high achiever in the performance category, but my raises and reviews were average each year. This career model was a big wakeup call for me, and it made me examine how I was managing my image.

As a senior project manager, I was assigned large projects, but the highest profile projects went to other project managers that were considered the best performers in the group. This annoyed me because I was highly competitive and thought that I had more talent than those other project managers. Also, I always delivered my projects on time and within budget, while some of my higher rated peers would regularly not deliver the same quality results.

The thought that 80% of my career was going to come from image was an epiphany. My higher rated peers were much more polished than me. While I delivered projects more successfully, they delivered a more professional project manager image. With their more finely crafted persona, these project managers also ended up getting better exposure through prominent projects. Exposure naturally evolves from a

1 – Image is Critical

great image, and they had that too.

To further prove the concept to me, another senior project manager in our group with mediocre skills advanced to a manager position after being in the company less than two years. During that time, she ran a high profile project that delivered late and over budget. Her quick advancement despite her poor skills showed that she was doing something very right, and I was not.

IMAGE IMAGE IMAGE!!!!!! It turns out that a great image is much more important than being a good project manager. I had to learn to be as successful at managing my image as I was at managing projects. I needed to master my image for better raises and promotions.

I started by reading a lot of material and attending many training courses on project management. Some of the material was interesting, but much of it was repetitive. One very expensive class (paid for by my employer) only provided vague theory and team building games. Another internally provided training program only succeeded in taking me away from the office for one week. Frankly, I was really looking for exact instructions or rules that I could easily use that would improve my image immediately, and I couldn't find it. I decided I needed to learn and develop those rules myself.

Everyone that I came into contact with at work could provide me examples of what to do and what not to do. I noted who wrote great emails and what made those emails effective. When people ran conference calls, what was appealing and what was not about the format? What bothered my very demanding boss about me? How were project estimates always too low and too short in duration?

In a short period of time, I was able to put together a comprehensive list of dos and don'ts for myself. Fortunately, they didn't include acting like a sycophant to my bosses. I was able to find methods that were only dedicated to increasing my image as a competent professional.

Following my new set of rules started to pay off immediately. Focusing on image management, my next large project was viewed very highly by management, and my performance rating that year was the highest rating. The following year, I was promoted to manager. Two years later, I was promoted to Vice President.

My performance also continued to improve over those years contributing to my success. I was able to create an amazingly simple estimating process that proved to accurately quote projects costing tens of millions of dollars. I was able to find ways to increase my project team's performance and eliminate critical project pitfalls with just a few straightforward rules. My increased use of a unique offshoring model cut multi-million dollar project costs in half while still delivering quality results.

1 – Image is Critical

This book lists 45 precise rules and instructions that I used to get back in front of my peers as a top project manager and get promoted multiple times in very quick order. I was able to master my image to create exposure to the decision makers in my company that ultimately led me to successfully manage programs costing $20 million dollars. In addition, many of the hundreds of project managers, business analysts, developers, and consultants reporting directly to me used these rules to rise through their organizations as well.

The first half of this book is dedicated to generating a positive and professional image for anyone in a business office environment in any industry. While it is written from the perspective of a project manager in a large bank, the rules can be applied by anyone that wants to impress those that are referred to as the "target audience" in this book. The target audience is anyone at a higher pay grade that may have any input into raises and promotions.

The second half of the book is devoted to superior project management rules that can't be found in any other book and will improve the image of your performance. Who can use these for immediate effect?

- Anyone that contributes to or works on projects of any type in any business
- Those aspiring to move into the project world because of the higher earnings of those generally employed in that area

- Managers and project managers that want to improve their project methodology

Great performance cannot be ignored as a contributor to your success. While most of this book is designed to enhance your image, many of the rules outlined here help you to execute projects more efficiently while also creating an appearance of superior execution. Unlike anything else published about project management, I will drill down to the few critical keys to deliver a great project and clear rules on how to overcome the most difficult obstacles.

When it came to offshoring, I pioneered large scale project development work for my company, but it took many years to evolve into the strategy that is further explained in this book. What started out only as development work offshore turned into huge teams of architects, analysts, designers, developers and testers working daily with onshore teams to bring in large software systems. Anyone involved with any type of offshore model will find the chapters on offshoring to be the most effective method in the world at guaranteeing quality results.

My model is very different than the standard model recommended by international consulting companies. One of the largest global consulting companies lauded my entire onshore and offshore team as one of the most effective they had in their company. Also, I consistently presented my offshoring model to many groups within my company because of its nearly

1 – Image is Critical

flawless performance for over 10 years.

Combining a top professional image with consistent performance will naturally lead to greater exposure. A vital factor used by management to determine who gets more exposure is how polished a project manager appears to be. An excellent metaphor is that parents do not want their children to make them look bad or embarrass them in front of others. Managers are not any different. Once management starts trusting that you present one of the best images with clients and others in the organization, they will trust you enough to put you on the most high profile and critical assignments. That is the path that ultimately leads to larger raises, bonuses, and promotions.

Rule 1:   Spend more time and energy improving your image than improving your performance

(Improved performance is a side benefit of more effective communication from good image management)

Get Back in Front

2

RESPOND IMMEDIATELY

The primary audience that you need to impress is the small group of clients and managers that ultimately determine your fate. While it is nice to be popular with other team members and groups that you have to deal with, they usually do not directly impact your image with management. You have to really focus on everyone that might have input on your performance review.

The most important act that you can do to impress your target audience is to show them that you prioritize their questions or requests, and then you deliver what they need quickly. You must respond immediately to them. And I really mean respond instantly!

Respond Instantly

Get Back in Front

Of all the advice in this book, this is the most important and one that you can use tomorrow. Think of it this way. It is a race between you and your peers, and the fastest to respond will win the largest raise or promotion. You cannot underestimate how this sticks in the minds of your target audience.

Utilize the same concept you already use to evaluate a tip for a server. As soon as you sit down, a server might immediately show up to ask for your beverage order. Then they might come back frequently to ask if you are ready to order. If the food is late from the kitchen, they will stop by to apologize instead of keeping you in the dark about its status. Afterward, she stops by frequently to ask how you are doing. The result is you might tip over 20%.

Now assume that the same server is delivering superior service to you at your table, but they are providing average service to a table not far away. How would you know? You wouldn't. At the end of your meal, you would be impressed that you just had the best server in the restaurant, whether it was true or not.

Many people are very hard to get a hold of. They do not answer their phone. Their instant message status is always "in a meeting," and they take a day or more to answer emails. They may believe that appearing busy makes them seem to be producing more than others, but it doesn't. It creates an image of poor time management skills.

2 – Respond Immediately

The following are exact rules to follow that will enhance your image as a quick responder with scenarios that you will encounter during your work day.

High Availability

One day, my new manager complained about another resource being hard for her to get a hold of near 5 pm the previous day. She said that people need to be available during core working hours. She really meant that message for me because I generally started my work day at 7:30 am and left at 4:30 pm. While my company had flexible work hours, she was telling me indirectly that I needed to be available from 8 am to 5 pm which are the hours that management expects me to be available. One of the most important images that you need to present to the work world is that you are easy to reach.

Start Time / End Time: Those in senior management generally work crazy hours. At the very least, they start at 7:30 and end at 5:30. That high availability is part of the reason why they got promoted to management. Many people have no choice in their work hours because they have assigned hours or they have child care obligations that they must meet. Others have terrible commutes, so they adjust their work hours to decrease their commute times. If at all possible, you need to start your work day at 7:55 am and leave at 5:05 pm.

Phone: Answer it every single time you can. Ensure that people can expect to get you when you are at your desk. Never set your phone to go automatically into voicemail unless you are on vacation because it will irritate your target audience more than anything else.

Desk Availability: Be at your desk as much as possible. Do not entertain yourself wandering around the office talking to co-workers. If you must chat, call them from your desk so that you can still answer the phone for anyone that calls. Arrange as many conference calls as possible instead of conference room meetings. It will allow you to run a meeting while responding to instant messages and emails. Face to face meetings are not usually with your target audience anyway, so you do not gain any political clout with them.

Stop What You Are Doing

The hardest part of the "respond instantly" concept is that you must stop what you are doing every time you get contacted by your target audience. It is natural human instinct to finish what you are working on and respond when you can, so you have to fight your natural instinct. You have to train yourself to refocus quickly, and you need to respond with a quality response every time. Never rush your response, and re-read any written correspondence three times before you click send.

2 – Respond Immediately

Instant, Phone, and Email Messages

Usually, the person contacting you knows if you are sitting at your desk through the instant message tool status, so you must start typing as fast as you can. Consider each instant message from your target audience as a golden opportunity to impress them. If you have to do some research before you can respond with an answer, you should react immediately with "I will investigate and get back to you as soon as possible." If you are in a meeting and receive and instant message request, respond with, "In a meeting, but I will respond shortly."

If you initiate the instant message, you need to always lead with a friendly greeting such as "Hi, Linda." The end of the opening message needs to finish with either "Thanks" or "Let me know if you need more information." While instant messaging is very informal, you need to add just a little bit of courtesy to the process. Metaphorically, you do not need to wear a three piece suit to work, but you need to dress really nice.

Most people believe that they are meeting formal or informal business rules if they return phone messages by the end of the day or within 24 hours. That is one of the reasons why most people get average raises every year.

Return your phone messages immediately. If you know that it will take a while to research information to provide a response, then you should call them back to let them know that you are working on it. Provide an estimate on when you expect to be able to answer their question.

While the measure of quick response with emails is a little slower than an instant message, it creates a larger opportunity to impress people. If you can respond instantly do so. If it takes 10 minutes to respond, then wait and respond when you have an answer. If you know that it will take longer than that to find out what you need, then you should respond with a message that you are working on it and expect to have an answer by a certain time.

Do not ever respond to your target audience informally, even if they do. Always start your email with their name at the top. Do not treat it as an instant message where you can quickly answer with a phrase. Make sure the response is well thought out and grammar is thoroughly reviewed. Consider that your email is being informally graded compared to your peers, so it must read better than theirs.

If it is a direct email to one person, put their name at the top followed by a comma. Then start the body of the email on the same line as their name. The goal is to walk a tight line between being formal and familiar at the same time. For example:

Alex, I completed the first draft of the project plan, and it is attached.

Thanks, Brad

---

2 – Respond Immediately

If the email is directed to one person with multiple people on the carbon copy list, put their name at the top followed by a comma. However, start the body of the text on the next line. You want to be more formal now because you are now including a wider audience. Here is the same email above when you have others carbon copied:

Alex,

I completed the first draft of the project plan, and it is attached.

Thanks, Brad

Accuracy

In your race to respond immediately to your target audience, you might make the crucial mistake of appearing foolish because you responded inaccurately. You will have destroyed the professional appearance you are trying so hard to show. Before you respond with communication in whatever form, you must slow down, thoroughly review the request again, and review your potential response.

Email is especially dangerous. There might be multiple requests in a single email, and the second request might be very easy to miss because it is not the main topic. Even harder to decipher is an email with a long thread that has messages from a number of people. In all scenarios, you must take the time to read every word so that your response is complete and accurate. A quick and inaccurate response will just make you appear rash.

Rule 2: Start your work day at 7:55 am and end it at 5:05 pm.

Rule 3: Respond instantly to anything from your target audience, even if you have to stop something else to do so

Rule 4: Slowly and thoroughly review the accuracy of every word in your reply before you respond

3

FINDING AND SELLING ENERGY

Finishing my sophomore year in college, I looked at my 3.0 GPA and knew that it must improve if I were to expect more job opportunities upon graduation. My grades were solid, but I knew I was underachieving and needed to find a way to improve by the next semester. People mature at different speeds, and it took me 20 years to figure out that I had to bring a lot more energy and enthusiasm to my schoolwork. I just didn't know quite how to do it.

There was one critical change that I made in my academic approach starting my junior year. I was not naturally motivated enough to just try harder every day and needed to find some easy ways to motivate myself. The main change that I applied was to sit in the middle of the front row in every class. I figured that forcing myself to sit right in front of the professor would force me to pay more attention because the teacher would be staring right at me every day.

If you are sitting right in front of your teacher and doodling or daydreaming, they are going to know it. If you hide in the back of the class, it is easier to ignore what is going on without getting caught. My first 15 years as a student were spent trying to avoid the teacher's attention, so I decided to toss that approach upside down. I now wanted as much of the teachers' attention as I could get. It wasn't that I really wanted to pay more attention; I needed to be forced to pay more attention.

My professors got to know me very well because I met with them regularly during their office hours to get a deeper understanding of what they thought were the highlights from the class material. I found out that teachers will often give you very obvious clues about what they will test you on during one-on-one conversations, so I was better able to prepare for tests.

My new approach worked brilliantly. By sitting up front in the middle, I stayed engaged in every class for the next two years. Since I was forced to pay more attention to the professor, I engaged in class discussions more. It made it much easier to remember the class material. Meeting regularly with professors helped me focus my studies on what they thought was a priority, and tests became easier.

Those simple tricks of putting me in the middle of the action made it easier to have energy because it forced me to be energized instead of just relying on my

3 – Finding and Selling Energy

internal drive. A realization hit me. Many people who I always considered really passionate about school were just really engaged. No wonder school appeared to come so easy to them.

My grades the next four semesters finished very differently than ever before. I earned almost straight A's the rest of the way, and the couple B's were in really hard classes where I felt glad to earn them. My last semester finished with the first 4.0 in my life, a big personal victory for all my hard work. I had raised my overall GPA to around 3.5. At that time, I started to understand that the rest of my career would require the same approach of finding ways to be energized and fully engaged.

Just Get to the Gym

There are an unlimited number of books and training seminars on motivational tools and techniques, and their only long lasting effect is to make a lot of money for the sellers of the material. Maybe the tips work for a week or two because they get people fired up for a short period of time. Their failure is that they rely on your inspiration to motivate you to greater effort and achievements. Staying inspired everyday is just not realistic. However, there is something simple that you can do to increase your energy without vitamins or famous quotes.

Some people are just wired with energy. They wake up at 5am, workout, enjoy their coffee and reading material, then go to work. They make the rest of us jealous, especially with their ability to get that workout in before their workday starts. Getting to the gym at any time of day is hard to do especially when life's responsibilities start adding up. Finding the time to squeeze in a 30-60 minute is usually not the problem. Finding the motivation to go stress your body for an hour when much of the rest of your day is spent battling stress IS the problem. Knowing how good those endorphins make you feel afterwards still doesn't sell you on the idea of going to work out.

One morning, I was trying to decide if I was going to work out at lunch that day. I had no excuse and hadn't been to the gym for over a week. Then a thought hit me. I needed to approach the gym exactly the same way I approached classes in college. I needed to find a way to metaphorically get right in front of the teacher and hope that the physical presence of being there would launch me the rest of the way. From that day forward, I completely changed my approach to going to the gym.

On the days that I had scheduled my exercise, I would routinely bring a bag with gym clothes for a lunch time workout. Approximately an hour before my scheduled workout, I would start arguing with myself to find reasons to not do it. Most of the time, I would still go workout. In the middle of the workout, the endorphins would kick in and feel great. How could I skip that pre-workout anticipation that would often cause me to skip so many days?

3 – Finding and Selling Energy

I stopped allowing myself to think about it. If I could just drive to the gym, the energy of being there would suck me in and naturally get me motivated. Motivating myself an hour ahead of time to go work out was counterproductive because my motivation would often fizzle out. No matter how tired or unmotivated I was, all I needed was to NOT think about working out and just get myself in the doors of the gym. That is a much easier goal than going through any mental exercise to get motivated to workout.

In both examples of where I placed myself in the classroom or getting myself in the gym door, I used the location to motivate me instead of having to rely on internal motivation. When looking for energy in the workplace, you need to find a way to put yourself in the middle of the action and the energy of it will take you the rest of the way.

Find meetings or improvement efforts that will force you to get more engaged in the processes that include your target audience or a wider audience that is unfamiliar to you. You will be forced to bring more energy into those meetings whether you physically feel it or not, and it is an opportunity to increase your exposure in the company. The ranks of management are filled with people who are adept at going to meetings and sounding intelligent.

Another good method to give you more energy in your workday is to sit right next to your manager or a group of higher level managers. Request that your cube or office be placed right in the middle of the danger zone. It will force you to stay on your toes and remain busy every minute of the day.

Reflect Energy

Observing the characteristics of people that make it to senior management can tell you a lot about what you need to do to take your career to the next level. One way or the other, they all graduated to a higher pay grade. In some cases, they just got lucky and were well liked by someone else that was moving up the organization. However, they mostly earned it because they all had the right stuff to get into that exclusive crowd. Sadly many of those in senior management are not very good at their job, but they all appear to have great energy and passion for their job. Do not be confused as you want to emulate their image performance and not their poor job performance.

A perfect example of the career benefits of great job energy came from the management group of a previous employer. The department head was hired into the company based on a superb resume and a great interview. He was a very intelligent guy that quickly learned and understood the hundreds of applications in his domain. He was very passionate about creating large changes across his organization, and he was great at communicating that to clients. His image was someone who was smart, energized, and engaged at all

3 – Finding and Selling Energy

levels of the organization. While all true, he was also horrible at his job for one key reason. The people that he hired were awful at their jobs, and they were never held accountable.

The second in command of the group was hired to manage a huge technology program in the group. He also had a great resume and interviewed well. While not as polished as the department head, he could really sell his vision of how the big changes were going to benefit the corporation. Years down the road, those big changes all delivered years late and tens of millions over budget. While this person was great at painting a vision, he was terrible at delivering it.

A third manger was hired by the first two to manage many of the projects in that huge program. He was not only extremely likable; his approach to every effort or issue sounded balanced and was based on common sense. It turned out though that every single one of his projects was a disaster. They too were all very late and over budget.

The last manager relevant to this group was the person hired by the other three to manage quality for the huge program. On the surface, this person brought a passion for quality unmatched by anyone. The level of detail that he could understand and communicate about was amazing. Unfortunately, the only thing he was good at was creating conflict with every other manager trying to deliver anything. Instead of improving quality, he just created distrust and discord in the program.

Ultimately, all four of these managers washed out of the company for one reason or another, but they amazingly survived for years. With their improved resumes and excellent interviewing talents, they all landed on their feet afterwards with great opportunities elsewhere. How do four very incompetent managers get hired and stay employed making a lot of money for a long period of time?

They all brought a lot of passion and energy every day to their jobs, and people buy what passionate people tell them. Sure, they also sounded intelligent, which clearly helps, but they really understood a key element of the image of leadership. Leaders get themselves out in front of others and assertively persuade others on their opinions. Passion and energy are winning attributes to selling yourself.

If you want more examples of how being passionate can sell your image, just look to political figures. Selling image through their passion and energy is the only real requirement of a politician. It is amazing that some politicians break the law and still get re-elected. People will buy into someone that exudes passion and makes mistakes over another candidate that has less energy.

Are you more likely to buy a car from a salesman who is passionate about his brand or someone who just seems nice?

Find Your Horizon Line

3 – Finding and Selling Energy

When staring out from a tall building or a mountaintop, it is easy to look to the horizon line and see everything in between. From the Hollywood Hills, you can see all the way to the Pacific Ocean and view Beverly Hills and Santa Monica in front of it. From the Empire State Building, you can see almost all of Long Island out to the beaches of the Hamptons with JFK and LaGuardia airports launching their planes in between. In any similar circumstance, it is easy to look to the horizon and track back from it. You could probably even start tracing the roads or freeways that lead to the horizon line. What is not easy is your vision of your own personal horizon line and the roads that lead to it.

Goal setting appears to be an easy task. Lose weight, get a great rating at the next job performance review, get promoted in two years, get married, start a family, buy a new car, and so on. If you were to list your goals, they would most likely be short term goals for the next one to three years. That seems reasonable, but career planning should look much further ahead. You need to determine what you want your life and career to look like 10 to 20 years down the road.

Most people in this world mislead themselves into believing that they are trying their best that life will all work out in the end. They just float down the river of life and expect that it will take them to a great place. Eventually though, they have regrets that they didn't achieve more, make more money, or pursue opportunity that others found. More specifically, most realize as they go through life that they need more money, whether for college for the kids, the desire to travel, or retirement. Regret is an awful thing because it is the recognition of opportunity lost from a lack of wisdom and initiative.

Finishing the next 20 years without regret is a pretty easy thing to do if you have the foresight and wisdom to set long term professional goals and apply initiative during that period to meet them. Sometimes it is hard to see the roads or paths that will lead you to your goals when you start, but new opportunities will come along as you consistently work towards them. If you do not achieve all your goals, you will still likely have achieved much more than you would have had you not been working towards anything. In a nutshell, don't walk blindly through life hoping the path you are on will magically lead you to success.

Rule 5:   Place yourself in places or opportunities that force you to get energized

Rule 6:   Reflect an image of a high energy person that's passionate about your job

Rule 7:   Set 10 or 20 year goals, and rate your progress every New Year

4

THE IMAGE OF TRACTION

There are always slow periods in any project or business activity. Sometimes it is caused by waiting for servers to be built, or it is often caused by everyone sitting around the room without a clue how to start a difficult project or effort. Whatever the cause, creating some type of momentum, achievement or progress each day will get you fractionally closer to your goals and create the appearance that the work effort is moving at a healthy pace.

How the target audience perceives you during those slow periods is what really makes a difference in your perceived image. It is critical that you are always seen to be producing traction at all times, whether it is really happening or not. Clients (internal and external) always feel that they are paying good money for a consistent effort, and that is what you have to show them. In reality, they may not be getting billed for much during a slow week, but all that they see is that nothing was done that week. Whether or not your or the team accomplished much that week, management and clients have to perceive that some forward progress was made in order for them to be happy.

Driving work and effort in a direction before you know exactly what direction to move can still put you on the right path to success. Inaction will get you nowhere. Here is a very good example of how creating traction without clear direction helped a very large project.

Senior management decided that they wanted to spend $20 million over three years on a new data warehouse. A data warehouse is a central repository of data which is created by integrating data from one or more sources. The project was assigned to me. A data architect consultant was hired at a very expensive rate to lead the design of the whole system. After three months, he quit, and I was left trying to figure out what this type of data warehouse should do and how to build it. I had 20 resources dedicated to the analysis effort, and they were all sitting around without anything to do.

My next step was to get everyone in a room and figure out what we were going to do next. As a group, we designed a strategy and documentation process that we would use to start poring through the mountain of data that needed to be analyzed. We also assigned resources to the various systems and files that needed to be analyzed. After a couple days, we were making good progress, even though we really

4 – The Image of Traction

didn't know if we were taking the right steps to get to the right place.

Several weeks later, I hired a more talented data architect consultant. He was very impressed by our progress and the large amount of data that we had thoroughly documented. It turns out that while we were just trying to do something productive each day, we spent $100,000 of the company's money wisely.

Often in business and projects, slow periods occur due to bottlenecks that are waiting to be resolved. When that happens, there are always documents that can be updated. Usually, documentation is the area that suffers the most in any project or effort because it is arduous to do and there often isn't enough time. These bottlenecks produce the perfect opportunity to catch up on those documents, and clients can be assured that the long term supportability of their effort is ensured with adequate documentation for support staff.

Another common scenario in projects is that team members often wait on phases to complete before moving on to major work on the next phase of a project. This is a really easy problem to solve because rarely does a project have to waterfall perfectly from one phase to the next. Development on one set of components can usually start while the designs of other components are still ongoing. Testing can often start while development is still ongoing with other components of the effort. A good example of this is when you take a test in school. If you have 1 hour to complete a 30 question test and you get stumped on the third question, are you going to sit there on the third question trying to figure out the answer while time ticks away? A good test taker skips the third question and continues on with the test and comes back to the hard question later if there is time. This way, you don't leave a bunch of unanswered questions when time runs out. The same holds true for a project.

Advertise Traction

If a tree falls in a forest and there is no one to hear it, did it make a noise? The answer is no (at least for the purposes of mastering your image). If you do a great job and only co-workers know about it, will that help your career? Will you get an excellent rating at your review next year? No.

No one likes people that go out of their way to be the boss's best friend all the time. Unfortunately, that method apparently works pretty well, but that is not me, and it will never be me. It is probably not you as well, but there is still plenty that you can do. There are two methods that can easily advertise everything good that is constantly going on around you, and you can do it without spending too much time acting silly around your boss or client.

If you are a manager or project manager, a weekly leadership meeting (reviewed thoroughly in a later chapter of this book) is the primary method to

4 – The Image of Traction

deliver how much you and your project team accomplished the past week. As the name implies, you and your key resources need to communicate directly to clients and/or management every week. Even small projects need a regularly occurring leadership meeting. Now, a weekly meeting of this sort is not an unusual event in project management, and many of you already have this on your calendar each week. However, your approach to that meeting needs to be different.

When creating an agenda, it should be written with the goal to highlight anything that might sound significant. Don't be afraid to make small but important efforts seem like your team just completed major milestones. Be creative, but don't lie. Of course, the agenda needs to cover important tasks and issues as well, but that should be your secondary goal. Make your regularly scheduled meeting with your target audience an infomercial for how talented you and your project team are. Accentuate the positives, and talk about the negatives as great learning opportunities that are enhancing work efforts going forward.

So what do you do when your key clients and other managers regularly skip your weekly leadership meeting? They often leave the responsibility to their staff to interact and get updates at that meeting. That is not an unusual scenario depending on the size and exposure of your responsibilities as perceived by senior management. They are evading your primary method to advertise yourself, but it is harder for them to escape your pursuit to give them a one-on-one update.

For clients and other key stakeholders that stay out of the loop, you need to call them up every two to three weeks and give them a five minute update on how much has been accomplished. You can lead your conversation with, "Hey, I just wanted to give you a really quick update on the project." If you keep the update very short, you will not irritate them, and you will have served three purposes with one call. One, you connected with them and for a good reason. Two, you advertised how much you and your team accomplished since you last talked. Three, you gave them an opportunity to give you feedback one-on-one that will often not occur in a meeting. If they do not offer feedback, ask for it.

Motivate Someone

Motivating a resource is easy, if you are their direct manager and deliver their annual performance review. For everyone else, it can be really hard. Roughly, 75% of resources working on projects in a professional office environment are already self-motivated. They are responsive, understand the team concept, and work well with others. Unfortunately, 25% of the people we work with slipped into the organization because of a good interview at some point or their best friend recommended them. For whatever reason, they continue to survive because their manager is

4 – The Image of Traction

incognizant, lazy, or indifferent to coaching them up to better efforts.

You have three options when it comes to making your sub-standard performers better. You can take a hard confrontational approach by bluntly letting them know that their production is sub-standard in the team and company. Another option is to find a way to get into their head and try to motivate them with praise. If either or both fail, then you have the best option which is to (metaphorically) beat them a thousand times with a baseball bat wrapped in huge soft pillows. You will have to bother them kindly for as long as it takes with a smile on your face and a consistent, courteous "please" and "thank you."

One of the greatest life lessons I have ever learned came from one of my favorite movies Shawshank Redemption. I know that it was fiction, but one particular scene helped define how I have approached my life ever since I first saw it. I hope I am not ruining it for anyone, but I have to divulge part of the ending.

The movie is about two men's survival in a terrible prison set in the 1940s. Near the end of the movie Andy Dufresne (played by Tim Robbins) escaped the prison by tunneling through a 30 foot concrete wall with a little metal rock hammer. His best friend Red (played by Morgan Freeman) described his escape with this narrative:

"I remember thinking it would take a man six hundred

years to tunnel through the wall with it. Old Andy did it in less than twenty. Oh, Andy loved geology. I imagine it appealed to his meticulous nature. An ice age here, million years of mountain building there. Geology is the study of pressure and time. That's all it takes really, pressure, and time."

What is stronger, the mountain or the river? At first, it appears the mountain because it stands tall and strong, an immovable object that looks like it will last forever. However, that river will wear it down to nothing more than sand and pebbles because of pressure and time. Stephen King and Frank Darabont wrote Shawshank Redemption and delivered a great life lesson on how to achieve anything, along with making one of the greatest movies of all time.

So how does that apply to motivating difficult resources? Your approach has to be patient and persistent. You need to be the river that wears down the mountain, but you need to do it much quicker than a million years. While you don't have gravity and friction at your disposal, you do have the power of irritation. Do not underestimate the ability to achieve anything you want by being mildly but persistently irritating.

There is a fine line between being aggressive and assertive, and you only want to be exceptionally assertive. The difference is how much respect you show towards the person you are trying to motivate.

4 – The Image of Traction

An assertive person shows tremendous respect while being consistent in the amount of pressure being applied. Every time you correspond with your difficult resources you need to be exceptionally courteous so that they cannot be discourteous to you.

Here is a good example of how courtesy impacts human behavior. If you are trying to merge into traffic and the drivers in that lane won't to let you in, there is something that you can do that will work every time. Either you or your passenger can wave at a driver of a car you want to pull in front of. Once you get their attention and make eye contact, you can point to the space in front of them which is a request to let you in. They cannot refuse because they know you got their attention, and it is personal now. You courteously asked to enter, and they cannot refuse. It is an unwritten social law: courtesy demands courtesy.

When reaching out to a difficult resource, vary the approach each time. Varying the approach will make it harder for them to completely ignore you. Start with an instant message, and follow up with another instant message three hours later. If that doesn't work, send them an email and carbon copy one or two resources on the team that are impacted just so they know they now have a larger audience. Next, go to the phone and leave a voice mail. If they are in your same building location, stop by their desk once in a while.

If time is even more urgent, the best approach is the short 15 minute daily team meeting in the morning so that each resource can give a quick update on the urgent effort that is late or nearing a deadline. You need to invite more than just your difficult resource or it will look as if you are singling them out, and it also exerts peer pressure on them to announce that they accomplished something the day prior. You can work it around a person's calendar, so they can't really reject it outright.

The goal is that you want difficult resources to finally give in and satisfy your requests just so that you will leave them alone. Your consistent courteous approach will drive them crazy, but they won't be able to lash out or outright refuse. It is also important that you consistently apologize for being such a bother, but you need to tell them that you don't have any choice because the deadlines are near or past.

Manage Your Boss

Studies have proven that people rate liking their manager as equally important to high pay for job satisfaction. Whether your manager is encouraging, overreacting, friendly, demeaning, micromanaging, or any other personality type, the place that you want your boss is far away, out of your hair and happy with your work. That might be hard to accomplish at first, but here are some rules to follow that will help take you down that path.

It is critical that your manager believes that you are on top of everything, and the primary way he will know that is by telling him. If you have a regularly

4 – The Image of Traction

scheduled one-on-one meeting with your boss, then it will be easy to spend some time advertising how much you accomplished. Similar to your weekly meeting, talk through an agenda of you and your team's accomplishments since you last talked. If you do not have a regularly scheduled one-on-one, then reach out to your boss once a week for an informal update. Again, you can lead your conversation with, "Hey, I just wanted to give you a really quick update on the project."

If you think that not conversing with your boss in over a week is a good thing, you are very wrong. You need to manage their perception of you instead of hoping they have a good perception of you. That can only occur with regular positive updates of the traction on your projects and efforts. You are training your boss to expect to hear from you on how well one part of their organization is running.

How much time and effort should you exert to becoming good friends with your boss? None, because it can do you harm. If there is a natural bond of friendship with your manager, go ahead and explore it, and it will likely pay dividends at review time. However, forcing conversation with your manager to try to be their friend might turn into a negative. Your manager will know what you are trying to do, and you might be irritating them even if they do not show it. Your image of competence will be more than enough to get you where you want to go.

The ultimate goal is to convince your manager

that they do not really need to manage you very much or engage your clients because you have everything under control. They know you are generating positive traction at all times and your clients or other stakeholders are aware of it as well. While you are convincing your manager to stay at arm's length, you are also keeping them fully informed so that they still feel in control.

Long Pole in the Tent

Many of the most high profile assignments or projects are small or medium efforts that have two or three goals that need to be worked simultaneously. In the planning phase, you must clearly identify the "longest pole in the tent," or the single most critical item that takes the longest to accomplish and/or creates the most dependency down the road. Then, you need to create instant traction as soon as possible on that "long pole."

Internal bureaucracy is always one of the longest poles. Getting full approval from a company to spend money always takes longer than it should, so it should be a candidate for extra attention early. Approvals for many other steps in company processes are also at risk to take longer because they involve people that are out of your control.

In technology projects, infrastructure builds are always one of the longest poles because of their highly complex nature and front-end dependency to be able

4 – The Image of Traction

to start any type of software development. Several times in my career, my teams built applications requiring ten or more servers of different types and a lot of infrastructure software tools that had to work in unison. Every time, getting the environment up and running took much longer than anticipated because there are just so many potential failure points. It wasn't from a lack of general skill by the infrastructure setup team.

The nature of infrastructure environments can be so complicated that it might be impossible for your team to know every answer on enabling the software to work together. The large companies that I worked for had an enormous number of resources that were very specialized, and there were still knowledge gaps. The only way to get to the end goal of getting the environment up and running is to grind through the issues every day. It can easily take two weeks or more to resolve a single issue. In these instances, schedule a daily meeting to make people accountable for daily traction.

I had a critical and very high profile project that had to be completed in six months. Instead of focusing on the charter and requirements document at kickoff, I had my team work on completing the infrastructure document first because it would likely take three months to get the servers built. While many questions on the infrastructure document couldn't be answered until the full requirements document had been filled out, it was enough to get the infrastructure team started so that the servers could be ordered and built more quickly. The project team was then able to complete software development on those servers the following three months to meet project goals.

Another potentially challenging project or business activity can be difficult or challenging resources or groups. Some people are just harder to work with than others, and they make everything harder for seemingly no reason. For example, I was leading the conversion of another company into our organization, and it required integration with a number of banking systems. Five of the six assigned groups were easy to work with and accomplished their work quickly. One group took three times as much attention from the project team and took twice as long to get their work done. They didn't even have the largest work set. To overcome this, we had to schedule daily meetings during the last two months of the project. Three members of my team, including me, were calling the members of their team every day to micro-manage everything. In the end, they barely made their deadlines but only after significant hand holding by myself and my team.

How can you keep traction with these challenging groups? It starts by swallowing your pride and not making them any angrier than they naturally are. Escalating issues to their management can cause your challenged group or resource to become even more difficult to work with. They are already bitter or lazy

4 – The Image of Traction

by nature, and being negative might make matters worse. They have survived long enough in your environment so they know how to work their manager anyway.

You must appeal to them almost daily to be more engaged as a team member, and then you must ensure that they get daily traction. Use that term directly with them over and over so that they start to understand what you are looking for.

Rule 8: If you are not sure what direction to go, choose the best option and get traction towards it immediately

Rule 9: Advertise successes to your target audience regularly

Rule 10: Identify higher risk tasks and get traction on those immediately and every day

Rule 11: When trying to motivate someone, be nice, sensitive, and unrelenting

Get Back in Front

5

MASTER BUREAUCRACY

When I was originally hired as a senior project manager for a large bank, it was in the middle of a massive expansion of their technology unit. The company was growing from a large bank to one of the largest in the nation, and it was almost doubling its technology group over a period of five years. During that time, it was going to go through a lot of growing pains. It was transforming from a place where you knew most of the people that you needed to deal with on a daily basis to an outfit that was engulfed by a huge bureaucracy.

In those early years, there were not a lot of standard processes or groups that could help a project manager get their job done. Project managers were expected to figure it out, and they were empowered to do it their way. I was a very entrepreneurial spirit that enjoyed doing things my way and networking with the people that I needed. Also, we were encouraged to take risks and deliver as soon as possible. For me, bureaucracy was a horrible thing that only drew attention away from the work that was needed and ultimately slowed project delivery.

As the company grew, more groups were created throughout the organization that ultimately placed a huge burden on the project manager. Database administrators were centralized. One information protection organization broke up into three different ones. Testing and architecture organizations were also created. PMOs (project management office) were formed. The company believed that these were a necessary part of doing business to standardize processes and skills within technology.

Each new group created more and more requirements for project managers in the organization whether you needed their help or not. Even if the architecture for an application wasn't changing, the architecture group needed to review large project designs. PMOs started putting meetings on my calendar regularly to teach us about the new technologies they were implementing. Every group had an extensive form to fill out in order to request resources. Soon, the 3 hours of time spent managing bureaucracy each week turned into 10 or more hours.

Worst of all, fast project delivery was being replaced by a culture of risk avoidance. Taking risks for quicker implementations gave way to taking more time to do additional testing. Getting rewarded for successful project delivery was replaced with a reward

5 – Master Bureaucracy

system for those that didn't have production issues. The Silicon Valley model of accepting failure to produce great things was now part of the past.

The change that was occurring was not symptomatic of just this bank. It was a standard model at most large companies. During growth, senior management starts losing touch with their organization, and they need to bring a very controlled and structured approach to every activity in their organization. Business units are more likely to complain about production outages than the slow pace of changes so an emphasis gets put on maintaining production integrity as opposed to rolling out the greatest technology for clients.

Instead of staying frustrated at all the new busy work that I had to do, I took a different view of the situation. The new culture appeared to reward those that knew how to manage the bureaucracy. Senior management was exclusively filled with people that had mastered the art of managing bureaucracy, and that was their primary job each day. I decided that I was going to become someone that was an expert at understanding the critical aspects of the new bureaucracy. Most importantly, I was going to build a connection with all the key people that managed or led the new organizations.

The effort that went into knowing all the key players in different organizations and forms to fill out really paid off. I started to become the person that other project managers were calling when they needed advice on how to advance their project. Management would ask me questions at group meetings about how other groups worked or who the key contacts were. My original thought was that bureaucracy was making my performance worse. However, it improved how others perceived my performance because I appeared someone that knew how to successfully navigate the company.

Mastering the bureaucracy in my company wasn't as hard as I originally envisioned. Before I changed my attitude, I would try to delegate as much of it to other members of my project team. Later, I made it a point to do as much of the bureaucratic wrangling myself at least once so that I would understand it and engage all the important people. Everything I learned was recorded in a document for my reference. Once it's learned for the first time, repeating the process does not take as much time in the future.

Becoming an expert at your company's bureaucracy will really impact your image with the target audience. Experts in navigating a company's bureaucracy are usually the ones that are relied on to handle the most important assignments. They are seen as the ones that get things done.

Rule 12: Become an expert at knowing who can do what in your company's bureaucracy

6

LEADERSHIP

Some people are born with special genes that just make them charismatic and likable. Growing up, these people always have a lot of friends and always seem to get treated better by teachers. They always date the best looking people and get great jobs. Once they become adults, they sell more or get promoted faster. The other 99% of us have to develop effective leadership skills that can ultimately allow our image to surpass those born with it.

Good leadership can best be explained with experiences in bad leadership. Everyone has had awful managers that were so bad it was hard to see how they survived in a manager role. My worst manager was a man who had a very likable and persuasive personality, so it was easy to understand how he got promoted to a senior management role. However, his management skills were so bad that he eventually was forced out of the company even with his gift of charisma.

There were two qualities that put him at the bottom of managerial competency. The first was that he really didn't set any clear direction for the team. He would lead meetings that would waste time talking about vague strategies that offered no clear direction. If I would choose a direction, he would criticize it without offering a better solution. The second problem was his inconsistency. I never knew from day to day what to expect from him. He would react differently to the same scenarios, and he would misinterpret events that would lead to fire drills. It was clear to me that he was in over his head and that he couldn't understand or execute his job with even reasonable competency.

Compare that experience to managers that are unlikable. Being unlikable doesn't mean that they are not good leaders. I have had managers that over react to small issues, never compliment good work, and do not appear to respect talent and abilities. However, they are consistent in setting up goals, responsibilities, and are predictable in how they react to challenges. If the unlikable managers were more appreciative and loyal, I would have thought of them as great managers. The differences between my terrible manager and unlikable managers are the key attributes that define good leadership.

Consistency is one of the most important leadership qualities for a project manager or manager. Being a consistent manager helps project resources be more accountable to you. It will create an

6 - Leadership

environment that allows resources to anticipate how you will react to situations and issues before they arise. Manager's consistency enables your team to take early action and be more accountable so you won't have to step in and solve issues for them.

Setting clear goals for the team and individuals is another key leadership quality. It is important to communicate goals as early as possible and repeat them as often as possible. Never trust that your resources are still tracking to the plan you set out for them one month ago because they probably aren't. Not everyone tracks to a plan like you want them to. Critical tasks and poor performers may require daily goal setting.

Knowing and assigning work to resources that match their strengths and weaknesses is a critical function of good project leadership. You have to learn who you can trust on your team with important issues/tasks and who you can't. The weakest resources on a team can usually be managed up to a level that makes them productive. If a resource has problems multi-tasking, then assigning that person three different assignments sets them up for failure. Burden your higher performing resources with multiple work sets, and ensure that your weaker resources are focusing on just one task at a time. A narrow focus will allow your weaker resources a greater chance of success, and in turn, helps the whole project succeed.

Once goals and tasks have been assigned to your

high performers, get out of their way. For them to be accountable, they have to be trusted that they can deliver on their own. Resources that know you trust and believe in them will work harder to meet your expectations. A project filled with leaders will make your life much easier.

Set high expectations at the start of the project. If people know more is expected from them at the beginning of the project, they will prepare to work harder and deliver more. Tell them that you expect that your project and team will be the best in the company which will really get their attention. Even if the team doesn't hit your lofty goals, they will still likely achieve more than you would have otherwise.

Great leadership requires complete support of every member on their team. You must be as accountable to each of them as they are to you and the project goals. Too often, project managers will be quick to use project team members as scapegoats when trying to explain why a project is late or over budget. Team resources eventually discover which leaders cover for them when they slip up and those that throw them under the bus when they don't. Loyalty is the difference between a good leader that can get the job done and a great leader that gets the most out of his team. Make sure your team knows that you are loyal and will "have their back" in all situations. In return, they will likely go the extra mile when you need them to.

6 - Leadership

> Rule 13: Be consistent in your approach to everything so that management and team resources know what to expect from you every time
>
> Rule 14: Set high expectations and goals for the team and individuals
>
> Rule 15: Assign weak resources only one task at a time to maximize their value
>
> Rule 16: Be very loyal so that others will go the extra mile for you

Get Back in Front

7 – Fire Drills

7

FIRE DRILLS

It is the day before a big implementation, and someone on your project team forgot to do something very easy that is now going to postpone the implementation. To remediate their error, it would routinely take about one week to get security access approvals and then a day or two of development. The timid will fold under this pressure and make the call to the boss about the need to delay the implementation. However, you can overcome this or any other challenge by following the rules below and expanding this to a fire drill for as many resources as you can. Quickly and efficiently overcoming fire drills really enhances your image as a key problem solver in your company.

The most important challenge for any leader is to generate the amount of internal energy that will be needed for the long day that is about to occur. When you receive bad news, it is emotionally deflating. To instantly turn around and start creating the "fire drill state of mind" in others will require a mental restart and focused determination from you.

The effort needs to begin with a conference call. You want to invite people to an urgent conference call without giving them a lot of information. Email is an easy way for people to reject requests or just deny any knowledge on how to help. Sending out an email to a large group is also a bad idea because a rejection by one person could cause the whole group to give up. The effort has to start on a conference call with requests via instant message or calendar invite to people to join this "ongoing and urgent" meeting. Once in the conference call, then resources can be told the full details of issue at hand. If they know all the details ahead of time, they might find a way to avoid the meeting because they know that their day might be about to be filled up.

The next goal is to get as many potential resources on that conference call as possible. You want it to become a fire drill for a wide audience as you cannot predict how someone that may appear to have a small part in finding a solution may become the key to the final answer. Even if a resource most likely can't help, invite them to the meeting because they might know a resource that can. Networking on the go is critical. If someone knows someone that might be able to help, ask them to reach out to that person to get them to join. Assigning tasks to people in a courteous way increases the level of accountability to a larger number of people.

7 – Fire Drills

A larger number of people on the call creates a public forum that naturally has urgency and peer pressure. You may want to portray the image that there is no other option than to resolve the problem. The more urgent that a problem appears to be, the more it will influence those that attend. Peer pressure is a great way to get bureaucratic walls to fall. Everyone that joins also has to understand that the call will not end nor their involvement until the issue is resolved.

Aggressively ask for resources outside the project team to do something. Often, you will pull in people that have the ability to make exceptions on an emergency basis that will be able to help resolve the problem, but they won't do it unless the environment is set up right. A very public conference call with a lot of stressed people is a hard forum for someone to say no when they actually have the ability to say yes. When they try to say no, you need to employ a standard sales axiom: "ask five times." Try to ask a different way each time, but you need to stay aggressive.

Lastly, a large group increases the odds that a creative technical answer can be found. The lengthy meeting will offer plenty of time to brainstorm for solutions. It needs to be an open forum for anyone with any idea how to solve the issue to contribute, and others outside the project team might have great ideas.

In a real world example, a very large project was scheduled to go into production for the very first time on Saturday. Senior management was watching closely because the project had very significant impact for some larger corporate goals. On Friday morning, it was discovered that a simple exception request had not been approved because the person that was responsible for getting the approval had forgotten about it. Without that exception or another solution, the project was not going to implement on Saturday. Getting an exception approved may seem like an easy thing to do, but in this case it required the approval of five people, and some were out of the office.

A large conference call was started. The entire project team attended as well as other groups that might have helpful ideas. Resources that managed the exception process were included as well. Initially, the exception resources stated that there was no way that the exception could be granted that day, especially since some of the approvers were inaccessible. The long conference call dragged on for four hours. After repeated requests for an exception, those in charge of the process found approval from higher management to grant the exception if a technical solution could not be found. Eventually, the combined team was able to help brainstorm a possible technical solution. In the end, the new technical solution solved the problem, and the project implemented successfully on time.

7 – Fire Drills

Rule 17: Get as many resources as possible to attend a conference call without giving full disclosure of the details of the fire drill

Rule 18: Keep the conference call going as long as it takes to resolve your file drill

Rule 19: Don't believe when people say "no" so ask 5 times in different ways

Get Back in Front

8

THE MEETING IS YOUR FRANCHISE

McDonalds has an amazing business model that taught the entire retail world how to operate. As it grew over the years, it set strict standards for restaurants everywhere from the style of furniture to the big arch outside in front. The food served inside the restaurant was also always the same from store to store, even though it currently serves local variants throughout the world. Everyone everywhere knew what to expect when they saw the golden arches.

To get even more detailed about the experience, science now knows that your brain ties together your senses with physical experiences. As your eyes see the McDonald's sign, your brain associates the taste experiences of the food and the sound of the soda pop fountain dispensing. Or, it also might associate the sound your children make when they hear they are going to get McDonalds. Considering their success record, those experiences must be pretty good for a lot of people.

As McDonald's grew, it became one of the safest franchises for investors in the world. A McDonald's franchise is as guaranteed as any other franchise to draw an excellent customer base from the moment it opens the doors. It has the least likelihood of going out of business. Investors associate McDonald's franchises as a nearly guaranteed investment in success.

Like McDonalds, you have to establish that your meetings all have the same format and are run the same way every time. The goal is to associate in attendees' minds an image of an effective, clear, efficient, brief, well managed, and well documented meeting. The meeting's imprint on attendees has an impact on how you are perceived by your target group. Your actions have to focus on making that reaction a very positive one.

Weekly Leadership Meeting

Your primary advertisement for your value to the organization is a weekly leadership meeting managed and run by you. The goal is to get as many of your target audience to attend so that you can show them how smoothly you can manage a high level staff meeting and drive your project towards success. Just like McDonalds, your attendees have to become familiar with a consistent and successful approach to managing a meeting so that they associate good

8 – The Meeting is Your Franchise

thoughts when they see it scheduled on their calendar.

The primary goal of your meeting is for the entire meeting to be short and efficient. Everyone loves a meeting that wraps up early, so make that a goal of every meeting you run. The only way to achieve that is to keep it moving as efficiently as possible. When a conversation drags on too long or starts getting sidetracked between two people, you have to say, "Those are very important points so we need to have more discussion offline."

What is a better format for a meeting; a conference call or an in-person meeting? Overwhelmingly, a conference call is a better option unless a key person in your target audience likes an in-person meeting. If your direct manager likes the team to assemble in a conference room then that is the right direction to go. Otherwise, always schedule conference calls for two great reasons. Everyone loves to multitask during a meeting and that is impossible with an in-person meeting. Also, members of your team that have urgent tasks on your project can often continue to work on them while conversation on the call does not involve them.

Opening a conference call should be a routine process so that regular attendees know exactly how it always starts. The worst way to start a meeting is to read off the attendee list to see who is there and continue to ask who just joined. It chews up a lot of time on the call and is contrary to our primary goal of keeping it short. The best approach to the greeting is to log into the call three minutes early to greet early birds. As folks join, ask who just joined, and greet them in a friendly way. Promptly at 2 minutes after the scheduled time, say, "It's two minutes past so let's get started."

Why two minutes? It gives attendees some leeway to call in a minute late, but it doesn't punish those who called in on time. At three minutes late, you are now starting to waste people's time. Also, if you announce that the two minute mark starts every meeting, all attendees will get used to that and they will know that you do not wait for late arrivals. Those that do call in late won't be offended because the meeting started at the same time it always does. Unless you are looking for someone to talk that did not announce yet, do not ask who may have just joined after the start of the meeting even for your target audience.

You must always have an agenda and minutes for every meeting that involves your target audience. An agenda is an obvious item for a meeting because it lays out the topics in the order they need to be discussed, and most people do review the agenda to follow along even in a conference call. However, most people do not review minutes so why do them? Minutes provide for a more professional image and help create the brand of a thorough project manager. It is the finishing touch on a great meeting.

The agenda should be minimalistic. It needs to look good and be an ad for your meeting. It should

8 – The Meeting is Your Franchise

only list topics so that it forces people to pay attention to the conversation. Many project managers like to send out detailed agendas that are too busy and look like minutes with a lot of information. Detailed agendas will cause people to read ahead and stop paying attention during the actual meeting. You want the entire group to be forced to pay attention to the whole meeting which provides two benefits. It produces a more engaged meeting, and it makes the meeting appear to be more engaged by participants. You want your target audience to view your meeting as a very active conversation.

Here is a list of items to include in the header section: project name, date and time of the meeting, teleconference line number or meeting room number, and a list of invitees. The body should only include a list of topics. Below is a good example:

Get Back in Front

CRM Replacement Project

Weekly Management Meeting Agenda

Date/Time	July 5, 2013 1:00pm-2:00pm
Teleconference Number and Access Code	866-555-1212 x3333
Invitees	Joe Smith, Amanda Stukely, Darren Brown, Sarah James, Robert Cowell

Topics

1. Completion of development servers

2. Business requirements review and signoff

3. Vendor negotiations

4. Software design

5. Offshore team

6. Administrative items

7. Open discussion

8 – The Meeting is Your Franchise

As you go through your meeting on your conference call, go ahead and type minutes under each topic on the agenda. The minutes should be the agenda with bullet points under each topic. Keep the minutes information short and to the point. It is less important that you capture every single thing anyone says and more important that the minutes look good and appear to be competent.

The following example of minutes provides a rough idea on how your minutes should look, but I would recommend you include much more detail than provided here.

Get Back in Front

CRM Replacement Project

Weekly Management Meeting Agenda

Date/Time	July 5, 2013 1:00pm-2:00pm
Teleconference Number and Access Code	866-555-1212 x3333
Invitees	Joe Smith, Amanda Stukely, Darren Brown, Sarah James, Robert Cowell

Topics

1. **Completion of development servers**
    - Oracle and application servers are fully installed;
2. **Business requirements review and signoff**
    - Review meeting has been scheduled by the business analyst
3. **Vendor negotiations**
    - Team members are scoring the different vendors
4. **Software design**
    - Application designers are 50% complete with design
5. **Offshore team**
    - Project leadership is reviewing offshore resumes
6. **Administrative items**
    - A meeting has been scheduled for next Tuesday with the CIO
7. **Open discussion**
    - The operations group has requested a demonstration of the tool

8 – The Meeting is Your Franchise

Let's review the key goals for your meetings:

1. Keep it short
2. Schedule conference calls
3. Start every meeting 2 minutes past the scheduled time
4. Greet only those that arrive prior to the two minute mark
5. Always have an agenda and minutes for meetings with the target audience
6. The agenda should just list topics, not sentences
7. The minutes should be written from the agenda

Be a Smart Attendee

How many times have you been in a meeting with management when someone said something stupid just to sound like they are plugged into the subject matter and smart as well? Do not fool yourself into thinking that you haven't done it once or twice, it is very easy to do. Mark Twain said, "Better to remain silent and be thought a fool than to speak and to remove all doubt." You need to remember that when you are sitting in a meeting with senior management.

For regularly scheduled meetings with management, you do not have to add something every meeting. A well placed contribution from time to time will be just fine for your image. No one wants to hear someone that compulsively has to add their two cents regularly. Contributing in a strategic way ensures that you appear to pay attention and are smart enough to know when you have something good to add or not.

Only a prepared speaker will be confident about what they are about to say. Giving a speech requires lengthy preparation. If unprepared, you will at some point start getting nervous and repetitive. Your important points will lose their impact and your audience will start looking away from you as your presentation becomes a train wreck.

When in meetings with your target audience, you need to approach it as you would a speech. You should be careful that you don't sound ignorant because these are the people that have a huge impact on your career. Most meetings come with an agenda so you should review that ahead of time to find a topic for you to speak about.

If you can, try to do a little research on whatever you are going to talk about so that you will sound really educated on the subject. The second and trickier part is how to contribute in the natural flow of conversation. Wait for a lengthier pause in the flow of the conversation to speak up because you will not seem over eager to contribute.

Rule 20:   Make all meetings an advertisement for how skilled and smart you are

Rule 21:   If you have to present a topic to your target audience, over prepare for it

9

EXPERT ESTIMATING

The next time you are rummaging around in your kitchen, reach into your refrigerator and pick up a full box of butter. Then, open your cupboard and pull out a full box of dry pasta. Put a box in each hand, and then close your eyes. Which one is heavier? Odds are you are going to say the butter. It clearly feels heavier in your hand, but it's not. Both are one pound, but your brain is playing tricks on you. Now that you know, go ahead and close your eyes again. The butter still feels heavier. You are not going crazy, but the reason sounds a little crazy.

The theory is called the size-weight illusion. Evolution of the human brain was influenced by our ability to pick out the right rock to throw at either our food or enemies. In choosing the best rock, our brain started pointing out the heaviest small rock because it turned out to be a great weapon of choice. Large rocks of the same weight just weren't as easy to throw accurately. To convince ourselves to select the smaller rock, our brain started intentionally fooling us into thinking it was heavier. More importantly, our brains were intentionally underestimating the larger rock for survival purposes.

Size-weight illusion is just one of a number of adaptive biases that has evolved in the human brain. Adaptive Bias is the theory that the human brain has evolved to reason adaptively to our environment instead of evolving based on rationale or truth. The theory says our brain will naturally ignore the data around us to fit some primordial instinct for survival. When translated into modern human behavior, there are a number of biases that can impact the project manager. Another critical cognitive bias that will negatively impact a project is called "planning fallacy."

Planning fallacy is the tendency of people to underestimate the time needed to complete a task, the costs that may be involved, the potential risks, and overestimate the benefits. It is routine for someone to estimate the most optimistic of scenarios for any endeavor. One good theory as to the cause of planning fallacy is that it is natural for someone to desire an outcome so that they will ultimately plan for the most optimistic of scenarios.

This lesson in psychology is to ensure that you do not completely trust your brain and how it perceives the world around it. It will play tricks on you and try to deceive you into thinking the road ahead is easier than it is. When you ask others for their estimates,

9 – Expert Estimating

they will also be deceived by their cognitive functions and produce estimates that are too low. Knowing that your psyche will try to deceive you, the outcome of the estimating exercise will likely be much too low and always needs to be increased significantly.

Whatever political gains are made with management from quick project time lines are completely dashed when projects take longer to complete. Almost every time a project takes longer than planned, additional work is involved and costs increase as well. Instead of being viewed as just bad at estimating, project managers are then viewed by the target audience as not capable because everyone agreed the estimates were good to begin with. Great estimates do not drastically improve your image, but bad estimates will ruin it.

It is much easier to explain why a project finished 50% under budget than 50% over budget. Both are terrible estimates but only one will get you in real trouble with management. A 50% under budget scenario can be explained away with words like "outperformed" and "surprised positive twists." Some unskilled managers might even laud a project for coming in so cheaply.

Top Down Estimating

The best way to estimate the costs and timeline for your project is to use the shared experience method, or clear examples from the past. The architects, database modelers, developers, testers, and analysts probably have had similar experiences at some point in the past, and the results of those efforts need to be the foundation for everything that you plan. However, it is not the staff's estimates of an activity that is important; it is the activity level on similar assignments that is the information that you need. Actual results from the past factor in many of the unforeseen events or risks that will likely be faced in the new effort.

If you ask a developer how many months it will take for them to complete a task, you will get an answer that is at serious risk for being too low. If you then ask how long a similar assignment took, they will likely provide an answer that is a much better foundation for an estimate. A person's ability to estimate the future is poor, but their ability to remember the past is pretty good. Shared experience is your best chance to arrive at accurate estimates, and it is far more accurate than bottom up estimating.

Getting back to the psychology of estimating, people tend to be overly optimistic about their future and like to deliver initial positive messages to their leadership. When a resource is asked to estimate an effort, they go through their mental task list or build a task list into a project plan. The resulting estimate will be a plan that is missing unknown variables or obstacles and relies on a best case scenario. If that same resource is asked to recall a similar situation, they will recall the final duration and work level of an

9 – Expert Estimating

effort that included all the unknown variables. The new project will likely have new or different unknown variables, but those variables will be similar.

If you are trying to estimate a very large project with a lot of development in new technologies, you will have to work hard at applying this rule. A large project can be broken down into smaller efforts that make it easier to estimate. If no one on your team has enough experience in the new technology to share experiences, then try to search outside your project team for resources that can help provide insight. If there is no one in your company that can help, ask a consulting company to estimate the effort based on their experiences. Also, it is rare that you would start using a new technology with inexperienced resources without having the software vendor involved somehow. Ask your software account manager to schedule a meeting or two with their technical resources.

Small projects are surprisingly dangerous to estimate because they are presumed to be safe because they are small. However, they can be more dangerous to your image than large projects for a variety of reasons. Management expects them to be easier to deliver on time and within budget because of their size. Many small projects can be high profile, critical to the organization, and have tight time constraints. The primary risk with small projects is that one small error in an assumption could easily double the cost and timeline.

Unlike a large project, any contingency built into a

small project is appropriately small. While it is less likely that a small project will have a major issue, the ability of any cost contingency to cover a major issue in a small project is non-existent. Ultimately, you have to estimate small projects with much more due diligence than would appear appropriate considering the size of the effort. Also, you need to consider investing more time in estimating politically high profile projects because one of those can make or break your reputation with the target audience.

The key component to top down estimating a small project is looking for risks in the project. Using the same shared experiences method, try to find as many hazards in previous examples and take the appropriate steps to mitigate them. The real goal of top down estimating small projects is finding and taking out all the risks.

Single Best Risk Reducer

The best way to reduce your risk in any project is to offshore as much as you can. It is simple math. The typical project adds up labor costs at internal rates and external rates for whatever a company has determined. Generally, internal rates range from $60 to $90 an hour in the United States. Offshore rates are significantly lower ranging from $20 to $40. If a big assumption goes bad in a project, it will take a lot of labor hours to make up for it, and it will be cheaper and faster to recover using offshore labor.

9 – Expert Estimating

Here is a great example. My team was building a $10 million transaction warehouse. It received files from 15 different banking applications and produced files for another 20 applications. One of the architects on the project completely misunderstood the scope of a large set of programs, and it was going to require 5,000 more development hours than what was anticipated.

If I had added 10 resources at the internal company rate, it would have cost the project an extra $400,000, a huge sum. Fortunately though, we already had a sizable offshore group on the project, and we were able to add the resources offshore very quickly. The cost was $125,000, and we met all of our original deadlines because we were able to add the extra resources in two weeks. The large offshore consulting company we worked with had a huge and flexible staff that was able to backfill our needs very quickly. The cost difference of $275,000 could have really damaged how I was ultimately viewed by my target audience.

High profile small projects have an even greater reason to offshore labor as a risk reducer because they are at greater risk to be considered a complete failure. A project with a $100,000 budget can add an unplanned effort of 400 hours for roughly $10,000. While a 10% variance on the project is not good, it is a lot better than an internal billable rate effort that would add $32,000. A 32% variance on a small project is considered a financial failure.

Many people do not like offshoring because they do not think it works very well. They argue that a 400-hour effort onshore would expand to 800 hours or more when done offshore. Yes, that is often correct. The average offshore program can be terrible and have tremendous pitfalls. Projects often take more effort and time because of many variables. However, the offshore model outlined later in this book will not extend timelines beyond what they would be with an onshore staff. A 400-hour effort with my offshore model stays a 400-hour effort when moving offshore.

Estimating Format

A spreadsheet application is my favorite software tool. It is the canvas that a project manager uses to paint his masterpiece. Nothing shows the time/cost model of a project quite like a first-rate spreadsheet. While a good project plan is needed for every project, a budget estimate will help tell the future tale of the project even better than the project plan.

No matter the project size, $20,000 to $20 million, a clear-cut spreadsheet can be used to best navigate your project. It needs to be simple, basic, and easy to update (examples on pages 79, 81-83). It needs to start on the left with a column titled "resource" that includes specific names or type of resource. Each subsequent column needs to be titled with subsequent months of the year, and the number in each field needs to match up to the number of hours that each

9 – Expert Estimating

specific resource is expected to work on the project. Where do you get those hours to fill in for each resource? You will need to use the shared experience model explained earlier.

How many hours do you fill in for each resource in each month? It depends on whether it is an internal resource or external resource. Internal resources do not tend to work more than 40 hours a week unless they are required for short periods of time. On a short engagement, it is also easy to build in days off including vacations. If it is a long engagement, just put in 160 hours per month per resource.

Consultants tend to want to work many more hours because they are billed hourly. Before a project starts, the number of hours that your company will approve per week needs to be established and capped. For the most part, consultants will work 45 hours a week or 180 hours a month, which also takes in holidays and maybe a vacation during a long assignment. Offshore resources also look to bill 45 hours a week if possible.

The right side of the spreadsheet has to wrap up costs for each resource. Once the last month column is completed, a subtotal column needs to add up the hours in every month. The next column needs to be the billable rate for each resource. After that, another subtotal column needs to multiply the total hours of each resource by their billable rate to arrive at a dollar amount. If there are extra fees such as travel and entertainment or other miscellaneous surcharges, those need to be added as one more column. The last column on the spreadsheet needs to be a total column, and the total column needs to be added to arrive at the grand total at the bottom.

Assume you have been assigned a small project that only requires internal labor which bills at $80 an hour. You assemble a team that includes an analyst, a technical lead or lead developer, and a tester. After reviewing the high level scope for the project, you need to ask each resource to give you an estimate based on a similar effort that they had in the past. Your analyst believes that it will take approximately two months working part time to meet with everyone and finalize the requirements. The technical lead that will be designing the effort informs you that the application team built something similar two years prior. The similar effort took one resource one month to design the software changes, two resources two months for development, and two resources one month for system testing. The tester thinks that it will only require one month of validation. Don't forget hours for the project manager role during the entire effort as well as trailing hours for all the resources that need to stay involved until the project is finished. Here is what that is going to look like on a spreadsheet:

9 – Expert Estimating

Resource	May	Jun	Jul	Aug	Sep	Oct	Nov	Total Hours	Rate	Cost
Project Manager	80	80	80	80	80	80	80	560	$80	$44,800
Analyst	80	80	10	10	10	10	10	210	$80	$16,800
Tech Lead			160	160	160	160	10	650	$80	$52,000
Developer				160	160	160	20	500	$80	$40,000
Tester							160	160	$80	$12,800
								Grand Total		$166,400

Bottom Up Estimating

Bottom up estimating is establishing the amount of hours for all the tasks in a project to deliver a cost estimate. A lot of project management guides will tell you that this is the best and most accurate way to estimate a project. That is not true, but it is an important piece of the puzzle. The top down estimate has to become (and remain) the primary estimate for the project while the bottom up estimate should be used for validating the top down estimate. The most accurate way to deliver a good bottom up estimate is with a detailed project plan.

When creating the project plan, the analyst, developers, and tester will each provide tasks and hour estimates for work. As they go through the process, they will assume that some things will go wrong and build a little more padding into their hours to ensure that they do not underestimate. When the project planning process is complete, you will usually find that the bottom up estimate is smaller than the top down estimate because of the psychology of estimating. Resources will regularly be overly optimistic about the time they need to accomplish anything because they are hard wired to do so. Even the extra hours built in will not overcome all of the obstacles they will likely encounter. The top down estimate includes a real world experience that consists of a likely larger set of obstacles that the project team will face.

What do you do when you find a disparity between both estimates? Almost always, the top down estimate will be the larger number, and you need to adjust the project plan to fit. You can increase major tasks or build in contingency tasks with dedicated hours. An easy set of tasks to include can be another round of unit testing or system testing in the plan. In the unlikely event that the bottom up estimate is larger, then it is easy to adjust your top down estimate to match.

Large Project Estimating

A $4 million dollar project is not any different than a small project. You can make your spreadsheet as big as you want, or you might want to separate years on different tabs. Also, you might want to separate the effort by types of resources on different tabs with a summary tab.

Larger projects will also usually have hardware and software costs included. These can be added into the plan as line items on the summary spreadsheet. Be sure to include those costs so that sales tax and shipping is included.

9 – Expert Estimating

Here is an example of a large project with many different types of charges over several tabs on a spreadsheet. This example spreads out the effort on three different tabs in your worksheet divided by external labor, internal labor, and a summary tab.

Get Back in Front

External Resource	Mar	Apr	May	Jun	Jul	Aug	Sep	Oct	Nov	Dec	Total Hours	Rate	T&E	Cost
Data Analyst	180	180	180	180	180	180	180	180	180	180	1800	$140	$40,000	$292,000
Senior Developer		180	180	180	180	180	180	180	180	180	1620	$140	$36,000	$262,800
Senior Developer		180	180	180	180	180	180	180	180	180	1620	$100	$36,000	$198,000
Senior Developer		180	180	180	180	180	180	180	180	180	1620	$100	$36,000	$198,000
Developer		180	180	180	180	180	180	180	180	180	1620	$85	$36,000	$173,700
Developer		180	180	180	180	180	180	180	180	180	1620	$85	$36,000	$173,700
Offshore Project Manager	180	180	180	180	180	180	180	180	180	180	1800	$35		$63,000
Offshore Developer		180	180	180	180	180	180	180	180	180	1620	$25		$40,500
Offshore Developer		180	180	180	180	180	180	180	180	180	1620	$25		$40,500
Offshore Developer		180	180	180	180	180	180	180	180	180	1620	$25		$40,500
Offshore Developer		180	180	180	180	180	180	180	180	180	1620	$25		$40,500
Offshore Developer		180	180	180	180	180	180	180	180	180	1620	$25		$40,500
Offshore Developer		180	180	180	180	180	180	180	180	180	1620	$25		$40,500
													Total	$1,604,200

9 – Expert Estimating

Internal Resource	Jan	Feb	Mar	Apr	May	Jun	Jul	Aug	Sep	Oct	Nov	Dec	Total Hours	Rate	Cost
Project Manager	160	160	160	160	160	160	160	160	160	160	160	160	1920	$80	$153,600
Business Analyst	160	160	160	160	20	20	20	20	20	20	20	20	800	$80	$64,000
Data Analyst			160	160	160	160	160	160	160	160	160	160	1600	$80	$128,000
Data Modeler				160	160	160							480	$80	$38,400
DBA				160	160	160	160	160	160	160	160	160	1440	$80	$115,200
Architect	160	160	160	160	160	10	10	10	10	10	10	10	870	$80	$69,600
Server Hardware Engineer			80	80	80	80	80						400	$80	$32,000
Network Engineer			80	80	80	80	80						400	$80	$32,000
Server Software Engineer				80	80	80	80						320	$80	$25,600
Senior Developer				160	160	160	160	160	160	160	160	160	1440	$80	$115,200
Developer				160	160	160	160	160	160	160	160	160	1440	$80	$115,200
Developer				160	160	160	160	160	160	160	160	160	1440	$80	$115,200
Developer				160	160	160	160	160	160	160	160	160	1440	$80	$115,200
Testing Lead				160	160	160	160	160	160	160	160	160	1440	$80	$115,200
Tester							160	160	160	160	160	160	960	$80	$76,800
Tester							160	160	160	160	160	160	960	$80	$76,800
Manager	10	10	10	10	10	10	10	10	10	10	10	10	120	$80	$9,600
														Total	$1,397,600

Project Summary	Cost
Internal Labor	$1,397,600
External Labor	$1,604,200
Servers	$200,000
Application Software	$400,000
Database Software	$150,000
Grand Total	$3,751,800

As you progress through the project and spend money, delete columns and adjust the spreadsheet as needed. What started as an original forecast will become your remaining forecast. When added to your budget spent to date, you will have a revised overall project forecast. Keep syncing your project plan hours to your overall budget as you accomplish milestones.

Anchoring

Anchoring is a cognitive bias describing the human predisposition to depend on the first piece of information provided to base all other decisions. When an anchor has been provided, people adjust all decisions from that anchor. More specifically applied to estimating, people will adjust their opinions up or down based on the first number they hear.

The retail housing market is a great example of how anchoring is used. When listing a house for sale, the seller creates an anchor price in potential buyers' minds. When the buyer determines that they are ready to negotiate on the price of the house, they start negotiations based on what the seller will ultimately sell the property for. The buyer won't ask for a purchase price that is half the asking price because they know that they will just likely aggravate the seller and cause them to eliminate any future negotiations. The buyer will submit a sale price that is designed to bring the seller down in price about 3% to 5%.

In regards to project estimating, anchoring can be a blessing and a curse. Often, the project manager will be pulled into an effort after the high level project discussions have taken place. There will already be a rough expectation of the cost and scope of the project. Once the project manager gets engaged, moving those numbers up to a more expensive and lengthy timeline could reflect negatively on the project manager's ability to deliver solutions efficiently. That is certainly not good for image management, but it is still necessary. Delivering late or over budget is worse than initially re-anchoring early in the estimating process.

Most of the time, project managers can have input in the early stages of conversation regarding a project, and that is the moment where you need to anchor your project. That anchor needs to be estimated as expensive and as lengthy as would seem reasonable because you need to protect yourself down the road. If the project is later re-estimated or delivered as less expensive and quicker than anticipated, it will create the image that you are great at project delivery. Your poor initial anchor will not be viewed as bad anchoring because no one that you work with has probably even heard of anchoring.

There are always a number of fire drills in every technology organization where some apparently small effort needs to be completed as quickly as possible. The following is a great example of one that could have reflected poorly on me instead of the great success it ultimately became.

External auditors had created a set of requirements that had to be met immediately. I was engaged in the earliest conversation around creating a solution. The client had not yet anchored the conversation with a date, but they were making it sound as if they needed a solution in three months. I sensed the danger because I knew that three months would only be a best case scenario, with five to six months as more likely. As quickly as I could, I stated that it would probably be a six month timeline while outlining the timing risks of the "long poles" to justify it. The client didn't argue with the timeline, but they asked for a compelling case to explain it to the auditors.

Once the auditors saw the milestones of the project timeline, they accepted it because they had now been anchored. While they required a solution as soon as possible, that ASAP became six months to them as well. As long as we had good traction and clear goals, they were appeased.

9 – Expert Estimating

The project took five months to complete, and it took a high level of urgency in the organization to get it done. Fortunately, I was viewed as overachieving and not poor anchoring. The client was thrilled that I had exceeded their expectations.

> Rule 22: Never underestimate your inability to estimate correctly
>
> Rule 23: Never underestimate anyone else's inability to estimate correctly
>
> Rule 24: Use offshore for as much project work as possible to protect your estimates
>
> Rule 25: Use your top down estimate as the primary estimate and your bottom up estimate as validation
>
> Rule 26: Be the first to anchor any project timeline or budget

Get Back in Front

10

MANAGING REQUIREMENTS

A project succeeds or fails during its analysis phase. Missed requirements are the worst possible obstacles that you could create for your project. Worse yet, it is self-inflicted damage to your image as a competent professional.

Have you ever heard the saying that a butterfly flapping its wings can create a typhoon or hurricane elsewhere? In theory, the very small amount of wind that a single butterfly creates has the capacity to trigger a chain of events that can ultimately lead to a devastating storm than can kill hundreds of thousands of people. The butterfly effect is an important idea in chaos theory. While it is mostly used to describe weather, it also has some important lessons for project management.

Very small differences in the initial stages of a project can mushroom out of control during the testing stage. One missing sentence in a requirements document could ultimately lead to major redesigns of key application functions which can result in project delays and cost overruns. There are always going to be some small requirements that will be missed and are out of your control. You need to ensure that your requirements document catches everything that you can control.

How can you mitigate this risk? How can you stop the hurricane from forming and destroying your project? There is one really great answer: Make sure your project uses a great analyst or group of analysts.

Great analysts are born, not made. They have a natural ability to easily focus their attention and write down exactly what they learned. Growing up, they probably paid close attention in school and received good grades. In the business world, the great analysts have the skill to listen to a complicated meeting and accurately capture what just occurred. Each day they can easily move from meeting to meeting and dissect each topic into their most important components while staying mentally sharp the whole time.

Great analysts need to be inquisitive problem solvers. As a project moves from the design phase to the final testing phase, analysts need to stay involved until the end because they uniquely understand how every technical solution solves every original problem or business goal.

Analysts that aren't very good will do one of two things to a project. They will either create a poor

10 – Managing Requirements

requirements document that will eventually create havoc during the other phases of the effort. Or they will force you to become the lead analyst because you no longer trust them so you will end up doing their job for them. Thus you will be working many more hours than is healthy for you, and you will be ignoring your primary responsibility of project management. Also, you might not be a very good analyst either.

Great analysts are forward facing with your clients and will have a dramatic impact on how you are viewed by them. They are the primary team members who spend a lot of time working with clients to figure out requirements. As the project progresses, they will be the primary person that answers the client's questions or resolves their issues. The image that your analysts reflect to your clients will also reflect on you. Analysts with a great image are perceived to have a manager that taught them well. Analysts with a poor image appear to have a manager that is lacking good leadership skills. The competence of your analysts will directly reflect upon your image.

Your career depends on finding and keeping great analysts. Unfortunately, it usually takes a full project lifecycle to discover who can be a trusted member of the team. Even if a requirements document is assembled professionally, you won't know until the final testing phase if an analyst really nailed down every major requirement.

The other members of your project team must be fully engaged in reviewing and approving any functional requirements document. During their review, they might also discover missed items. A final approval by each team member means they understand the requirements and are now accountable for those requirements.

Never Volunteer Requirements

In 1987, I was 18 years old and enlisted in the U.S. Army. It was an invaluable learning experience. As my first time away from home, I was incredibly homesick, and I was learning to survive in a tough situation that I had inaccurately depicted in my mind. It taught me how to live with and adjust to many types of people that grew up in environments very different than my classic suburbia upbringing. The most important lesson I learned from the Army was that volunteering can have very negative consequences.

I volunteered for anything I could in an effort to impress the Drill Sergeants. Instead of amazing them, I was only rewarded with awful opportunities to do extra labor that ultimately had no benefit to me. It turned out that they really didn't care who was trying too hard to look good. They could easily see through that charade. They were more impressed with the soldiers who best completed their standard goals each day.

Technology is an area that has tremendous opportunity for disaster. The more you try to impress others with how much you can help your company,

10 – Managing Requirements

the more you will hurt yourself and your company. Do not try to create solutions where there are no internal or external clients creating requirements for you to do so. Focus on creating the image that you are superior at delivering the requirements that they asked for, and no more.

An experience I had on a project is a great example of what not to do. My business client had the need to add a lot of options on an application that was vital for their business operations. Our bank had an old application that was still doing a decent job, but the application vendor was no longer investing much money in the product. While it worked well, it would have required significant customization to meet the new requirements. What followed was the worst decision of my project management career.

What I should have done was create a $1 million dollar project and drawn a straight line between the requirements and a large set of customizations. It would have delivered everything the client asked for and the cost was reasonable. The project timeline would have been approximately one year, which would have made the client happy. Instead of this good decision, I promoted an alternative in hopes of further impressing the client.

There appeared to be three good options. The first was a set of updates from our current application vendor that could be added to the current system. The second option was a new vendor that wanted to sell us a new software application that we would have to install and then spend a lot of time getting to work in our environment. The third option was the most intriguing. A different vendor was proposing that the whole application be outsourced to them.

The third vendor was an international company that already had a tremendous presence and good reputation in that field. Their pricing created a much better business case than option number two, and they had a large technical team of experts that they said would make the effort easy. Unfortunately, the price of the project would be $3 million, which was three times as much as the first option.

I recommended to senior management that the best decision was to go with option number three because it was in the long term strategic interest of the company. At the time, I believed it was the right call even though the long term requirements were not clearly defined enough to have made a decision as such. Additionally, a successful outcome would really impress senior management. They decided to go with my recommendation.

The project had now tripled in size and complexity despite no real business requirements to do so. I had staked a big part of my reputation on this business decision, and it really had to deliver. The vendor's skillful sales team and excellent international reputation made this appear to be the easiest large project I ever had. I was wrong.

Instead of negotiating and finalizing a contract with

10 – Managing Requirements

the vendor, I should have had a trial test to prove that they could at least deliver a little of what they promised, but I didn't. Instead, I found out the hard way that the vendor oversold their capabilities and underestimated their ability to catch up quickly. The proof of concept ended up taking six months longer than scheduled. Thankfully, the contract was fixed bid so the costs were contained, but it was off to a rough start.

Midway through development of the proof of concept, the bank went through a massive cost cutting effort and most large projects were cancelled. My project was cut, but it was unrelated to its ongoing challenges. I was saved from having to continue that project with an inept vendor.

There were three options, I picked the one that I THOUGHT my client would be most dazzled with but I was wrong. I should have just met their requirements, and they would have been happy.

Saving a Project

At some point in my career, I was identified by management as the best person in the group at managing projects. My manager told me about another project of his that was in the testing phase that was failing, and he asked me if I could help try to fix it. Thinking that this was a great opportunity to prove how valuable I was, I agreed. I was confident that I could turn it around. The project required building a new application that could examine transaction data and flag various high risk suspicious items.

Attending the daily meetings that worked through defects, I was able to get a good understanding of the resources on the project. While the project manager was in a little bit over her head, she was managing the testing process adequately. The lead developer was fairly intelligent, and was able to solve issues quickly. The rest of the team appeared to be generally competent. There were no glaring red flags that I could easily identify.

At the end of my first two weeks on the project, I discovered that there was a major missed requirement that would require two extra weeks of development to remediate. Soon, another missed requirement was discovered. By the time testing was completed, there were five major missed requirements discovered that delayed implementation by eight months. When I started helping with testing, my goal was to improve their testing process. It turned out that their testing process was already in decent shape, and I didn't add a lot of value. My error was thinking that I could come into a testing phase of a project and get everything fixed. In other experiences, I had stepped into projects struggling with their testing process and had been able to improve those quickly. In each of those cases, the day to day management of the defect process was broken and needed micromanagement of the process to improve. This project was different.

10 – Managing Requirements

It was impossible to fix this project. The analyst, project manager, and client did a poor job establishing the requirements, and it made it impossible for the project to meet predictable timelines. The development team provided budget and timing estimates based on faulty requirements. The project was doomed to failure because the requirements process was so poorly executed. Forecasts are only able to be made from what is in the requirements document, and missing requirements will never lead to a good outcome.

There is only one thing you can do if you find yourself in a similar situation. As soon as a major missing requirement is found in a project, a full re-review of the requirements has to be completed. It may take time away from testing for some of the resources, but it is necessary to do a health check of the requirements document. The sooner you find out everything that is missing in the requirements, the sooner you can re-plan the project. It is better to tell senior management the project will be delayed by six months than to tell them every month that you need another two months.

Rule 27: Make sure your requirements document is as complete as possible because missing requirements will destroy a project

Rule 28: Never add requirements that the client isn't asking for

Rule 29: Ensure that "nice to have" items are never included in a requirements document

Rule 30: Communicate to every member of your team that they will be held accountable to the requirements document so they need to meaningfully participate in the process

Rule 31: Avoid at all costs any assignment requesting you to save a project

11

PROJECT PLANNING SIMPLIFIED

Project plans are essential for managing a great project and shows your target audience that you have a clear roadmap for the effort. In project management, detailed plans are a required tool of the trade, and most are produced using Microsoft's Excel or Project or a similar software product. Many companies have internal applications that work in the same fashion and tie actual hours worked into the plan. The creation of and continued maintenance of project plans though can become an all-consuming activity if not done properly. The primary goal of a project plan should be to create an image of a great road map for your project while taking up as little of your time as possible.

At the start of any project, your project plan will need to be published to your target audience to prove that you have a solid plan of attack and can validate hour estimates for budgeting purposes. It is possible that some of them might review it for quality at that point. As the project progresses though, it is unlikely anyone without tasks in the plan will review it because it takes a lot of energy to review and understand a large plan. It becomes more of a tool for the project team than a communication tool to your larger audience, so focus on keeping it updated for those that have tasks remaining. The other reason that your plan will get little attention from the target audience is that you will keep people focused on a regularly published Gantt chart that is explained later in this chapter.

The detail that goes into your project plan will depend on the size of your project. With small projects, it will be easy to build out tasks that can be listed down to 4 hours or less. It is the large projects that are much trickier. Tasks need to reflect major components instead of small individual tasks. Tasks still need to be listed as a number of hours, but they need to be grouped together to include multiple days/multiple resources if possible, and combined into a single task.

In an example on page 102, a small project that requires 2 developers for website changes should be outlined in a project plan at a granular level. One task each should be assigned to each developer's stage of work. One task should be assigned to the first resource working on the front end design changes to the website. The first task should be design, and the next tasks should be development, unit testing, system testing, integrated testing, and user testing. The second resource that is working on the middle layer of application code should also get five tasks assigned as well. The plan now has 12 tasks for those two resources.

If that small project work effort is combined into a large project, you need to combine and shorten the whole plan from twelve tasks to four, excluding header tasks. The overall work set of front end and middle layer can be combined into a single set of tasks instead of two where the resources are both listed for each task. Design needs to be a single task. Development and unit testing can be combined into just development. System and integrated testing should be combined into just system testing. User testing needs to stay the same.

Using Microsoft Project or a similar tool is the optimal choice for project planning with Excel or similar tool as a good backup. You need to KISS your project plan, or Keep It Simple Stupid. While Microsoft Project may be able to give you 1,000 options for the plan, you only need seven key data columns. The more information you build into it will require an exponential amount of work to update it. Build it with only these seven data elements or columns: ID, Task, Start Date, End Date, Hours, % Complete, Resources. The following is an example of two different ways to display what is outlined above. Don't forget to roll up hours and dates to header rows.

Small Project:

ID	Task	Start Date	End Date	Hours	% Complete	Resources
1	Website Changes	2/1/2014	6/3/2013	1160	0%	Dan, Jan
2	Front End Changes	2/1/2014	5/31/2014	560	0%	Dan Smith
3	Design	2/1/2014	2/14/2014	80	0%	Dan Smith
4	Development	2/15/2014	3/14/2014	160	0%	Dan Smith
5	Unit Testing	3/15/2014	3/31/2014	80	0%	Dan Smith
6	System Testing	4/1/2014	4/14/2014	80	0%	Dan Smith
7	Integrated Testing	4/15/2014	4/30/2014	80	0%	Dan Smith
8	User Testing	5/1/2014	5/31/2014	80	0%	Dan Smith
9	Application Layer Changes	2/1/2014	5/31/2014	560	0%	Jan Brown
10	Design	2/1/2014	2/14/2014	80	0%	Jan Brown
11	Development	2/15/2014	3/14/2014	160	0%	Jan Brown
12	Unit Testing	3/15/2014	3/31/2014	80	0%	Jan Brown
13	System Testing	4/1/2014	4/14/2014	80	0%	Jan Brown
14	Integrated Testing	4/15/2014	4/30/2014	80	0%	Jan Brown
15	User Testing	5/1/2014	5/31/2014	80	0%	Jan Brown
16	Implementation	6/1/2014	6/3/2013	40	0%	Dan, Jan

Here is the same effort listed as a component of a large project:

ID	Task	Start Date	End Date	Hours	% Complete	Resources
1	Website Changes	2/1/2014	6/3/2013	1160	0%	Dan, Jan
3	Design	2/1/2014	2/14/2014	160	0%	Dan, Jan
4	Development	2/15/2014	3/14/2014	480	0%	Dan, Jan
6	System Testing	4/1/2014	4/14/2014	320	0%	Dan, Jan
8	User Testing	5/1/2014	5/31/2014	160	0%	Dan, Jan
16	Implementation	6/1/2014	6/3/2013	40	0%	Dan, Jan

Most companies require input of projects into a tool or application that ties it into actual hours worked. You may be required to also install the detailed plan into it as well. If that occurs, try to design it to only track these seven data elements or the fewest number of data elements possible. The more frivolous data you track in your project plan increases the amount of worthless busy work you will spend

11 – Project Planning Simplified

updating your plan.

Gantt Charts

Henry Gantt was a mechanical engineer and management consultant that was way ahead of his time. While the world was working on the mass produced automobile and airplane, Henry was creating business process improvement techniques in the early 1900s. Ultimately, his name would live on with his greatest contribution, the Gantt chart that he created around 1910. The Lawrence Henry Gantt medal was created in 1929 by the American Society of Mechanical Engineers (ASME), and it continues to this day. It is for contributions for management and community service.

The primary way to tell the story of your project to your target audience and project team needs to be using a Gantt chart. It is a bar chart that visually describes a project schedule. It takes the dates in a project schedule and lays them out in a method that is easier to read and understand. It has the ability to tell a viewer the future story of the project in seconds what might normally take an hour if reviewing just a project plan without a Gantt chart. Most project management tools like Microsoft Project include Gantt charts as a standard part of the basic project plan.

There are three reasons you want to use a Gantt chart as your primary tool to display your project timelines. The first reason is that it is easy to update and get quick review and acceptance from others. The second reason is that everyone likes a Gantt chart versus having to look at a project plan. The third reason is that it allows you to be a little lazy on your project plan. Since large project plans can take up so much time, you need a weekly project activity that can slide during very hectic times, and that should be your time intensive project plan. As long as your Gantt chart is updated regularly, and everyone is pushing for those milestone dates, you will rarely get a request from management to review the details of your project plan. Your Gantt chart acts as your image enhancing plan for your target audience.

While every project management software tool includes Gantt charts, you should build your own in Microsoft Excel or a similar tool. It will ultimately take you less time to update because the Gantt charts in the project tools require the project plan to be fully updated in order for the Gantt charts to be updated accurately. With Excel, you can create a simple and easy to update chart for your audience.

Here is an example of a Gantt chart for the small project defined earlier in this chapter for website changes:

11 – Project Planning Simplified

Website Changes	Feb	Mar	Apr	May	Jun
Front End Changes					
Design					
Development					
Unit Testing					
System Testing					
Integrated Testing					
User Testing					
Application Layer Changes					
Design					
Development					
Unit Testing					
System Testing					
Integrated Testing					
User Testing					
Implementation					

Design
Development
Unit Testing
System Testing
Integrated Testing
User Testing
Rollout

Notice how the chart has a legend at the bottom and April is centered over five columns. That represents the five weeks in April in 2014, or the fifth weekday that has three of the five days in April. For small projects, your Gantt chart might align so closely with the project plan that you can actually substitute it for the project plan.

Here is the same Gantt chart for the example of the same effort as a component in a larger project:

	Feb	Mar	Apr	May	Jun
Website Changes					
Design					
Development					
System Testing					
User Testing					
Implementation					

Design
Development
System Testing
User Testing
Rollout

Rule 32: Use Gantt Charts to communicate your project plan to your target audience

Rule 33: Do not get bogged down spending too much time managing too many tasks in your project plan

Rule 34: Avoid frivolous data in your project plan because it will take time away from effective leadership

12

EVERYONE IS A PROJECT MANAGER

If you always feel like you are overwhelmed and have too much to do, you have some wonderful options to get out of that 50+ hours per week trap. Every person on your project needs to become a project manager regardless of their job description or title. You need to become a master delegator and assign as much day-to-day task management work as you can onto your project team members. The more bureaucratic work that you can take off your plate, the more time you will have to resolve issues and drive traction on your projects. In addition to helping reduce your stress, it will also significantly increase the quality of your project and enable more time to manage your image with your target audience.

At the beginning of every project, communicate to every member of your project team that they will be held accountable to the project as a whole, and they will have project management goals on top of their assigned job. It is best that you make this announcement at one big meeting because there will be natural acceptance by the group. When people feel that the group has bought into a concept, individuals usually accept it. However, if you try to deliver that message personally to each member of your team, they might tell you outright that they disagree.

In that group meeting, communicate that every resource will be expected to take on small project management tasks. They will be required to create components of the project plan using whatever tool they have such as Microsoft Excel. Training them to use more sophisticated project planning software may be going too far. They will be expected to add items to the issues lists and risk documents on their own without expecting the project manager to always do it. They might have to schedule and lead small meetings, including agendas and minutes.

Weakest Link

An immediate benefit of using your project team resources to help with bureaucratic tasks is to enable the project manager to do more managing. Updating project plans, issues lists, agendas, minutes, and internal applications built for project management can consume a full week. Instead, it is critical that project managers spend most of their time dedicated to probing and fixing the weak spots in the project. In general, you will spend roughly 80% of your time working with the weakest 20% of your project team, or the 80/20 rule. If you do not directly manage the weak resources on your team, they will fail at meeting some of their goals, and so will the whole project.

The weakest link of the chain metaphor is pretty good, and it applies perfectly to a project team. If one resource on a project team produces poor quality and late work, then the entire project plan can be impacted. Never trust the estimates of your weakest link. Keep them focused on one effort at a time because their biggest talent deficiency is most likely multi-tasking and time management. Make them prove everything they do, and review their output every day.

Building Accountability

If you asked 20 members of a project team what accountability means, you would get 20 different answers. Unfortunately, most of them will define accountability to their very specific defined role and not to the overall success of the project. What you would prefer to hear is that accountability can be defined equally as achieving their defined role and the overall success of the project. Even if you could get each of them to admit that your definition was better than theirs, most won't take initiative to do everything they can to make sure the project succeeds.

By assigning every project team member a sub-role as "junior project manager," they will accept that they will be judged by the overall results of the project as well as their individual task assignments. They need to expand their concerns to take initiative, without being told, when they see something that needs improvement. When everyone commits to goals larger than themselves, great things happen.

Make Time for Politics

For many years, I have always said to my project teams that one of my key responsibilities was CPO, or Chief Political Officer. I explained that my job was to protect all of them by advertising how good they were and deflect any criticisms from them as a team. Those activities take time.

If you get too bogged down with busy work, you will not have time for the crucial aspect of your job which is to master your image in project management. Many of the rules and instructions in this book take time to execute, and those must be prioritized in your day-to-day responsibilities. That is why you need to make everyone on your team a junior project manager.

> Rule 35: At the onset of any project, make sure that everyone knows that they have two jobs: project manager and their official assignment
>
> Rule 36: Find and dedicate at least 10 minutes every day to market your image

13

THE POLITICS OF OFFSHORING

In the United States, offshoring is very popular with technology organizations as a great way to save huge amounts of money while still delivering production support and project objectives. To the rest of the country, it is a dirty word that people associate with American workers losing their jobs to predatory nations from around the world. Unfortunately, the overwhelming abuse by China of trade with the U.S. has clouded everyone's view of offshoring.

There is no question that what has occurred in China over the past 23 years is a miracle, lifting hundreds of millions of people out of poverty. It was able to transform itself into an economic powerhouse and primary manufacturer for the world. The political climate in China has also evolved somewhat from the horrific Tiananmen Square massacre to a (non-democratic) government that hands over power every ten years to a more economically progressive group that worries about job creation for the masses.

In 1990, China had a trade surplus with the U.S. of approximately $10 billion. In 2012, that number had grown to approximately $315 billion which is more than half of the overall trade deficit of the U.S. That is an enormous amount that impacts every American in some way from consumers shopping in Walmart to those who lost their jobs when their manufacturing plant in Ohio left for China. What was a key contributor to this tremendous surge of imports? China cheats, and the U.S. government does little about it.

The primary way that China cheats is that it manipulates its currency, roughly pegging it to the U.S. dollar. It does that by buying U.S. Treasuries to depress the value of the Chinese Yuan. Ultimately, it depresses the real cost of its products that it exports to the United States creating an unfair advantage against U.S. manufacturers. What started in 1990 and accelerated in 2000 is that U.S. companies moved their manufacturing plants to China or started contracting with Chinese companies to produce their products. Walmart went from advertising "Made in the USA" product lineup in the 80s to encouraging suppliers to switch to Chinese manufacturing to save pennies per product on their wholesale costs. It appeared to American consumers that all U.S. manufacturing went to China overnight.

Going forward, China is slowly appreciating the Yuan against the dollar, and they have long term plans

13 – The Politics of Offshoring

to make the Yuan a real floating world currency. China has plans to increase foreign and private enterprise within their economy as well. The U.S. also discovered it had access to almost unlimited quantities of natural gas through the use of fracking which is bringing manufacturing back to the U.S. because of cheap energy costs. So while the future appears that a rebalance of trade between the U.S. and China might occur, the damage to the reputation of offshoring is already done.

India

India is the dominant nation in the realm of technology offshoring. It has a roughly 60% share of the world market, and the rest of the market is generally split between the Philippines, Brazil, Mexico, Vietnam, and eastern European countries. Focusing on India, it has roughly a $15 billion dollar trade surplus with the U.S. with imports running at 50% of exports. In comparison, U.S. exports to China are only about 25% of imports. Also, India only contributes less than 3% of the overall U.S. trade deficit when China is running over 50%. Trade with India is more reciprocal than trade with China, and it is not damaging GDP growth like China is.

The national currency of India is the Rupee, and it floats on the world market. As India gets wealthier, the Rupee appreciates in value, and it takes more dollars to hire offshore contractors. It has the effect of making India less competitive as a destination for offshoring. While India is a difficult but improving market for U.S. products and companies, the offshoring of technology labor to India follows normal trading economics.

Companies love the cost savings and extra production that offshoring to India provides, but the average person in the U.S. doesn't like what it means for American jobs. That way of thinking extends somewhat to the employees of corporations that are tasked with the requirement of offshoring their support and project development. The vast majority of technology managers and project managers in the U.S. has a very bad perception of offshoring and try to avoid it as much as they can, even when their company requires it.

Another key reason that American technology managers don't like offshoring is that they are not used to dealing with people from different cultures. While all Indians that work in the technology space are fluent in English, the pace of communication is different between Americans and Indians. American clients are very forceful in their opinions and assertive in conversation, and Indian consultants are very patient. Americans often incorrectly perceive that the lack of assertive opinions by offshore teams is from a skill and expertise deficit. Instead of getting ahead of issues, managers wait until project deliverables are not met and then blame the Indian vendor.

Besides cost benefits, offshoring from the U.S. is

13 – The Politics of Offshoring

going to continue to grow because the U.S. may not produce enough technology professionals over the next 10 years to fill demand. The forecast for the number of technology jobs needed by U.S. companies is expected to increase 30% from 2013 to 2020 according to the U.S. Bureau of Labor Statistics. Consider that the unemployment rate in the technology area is currently 3.4% (as of the date of this book being published) while the overall unemployment rate is 6.7%. As the U.S. economy continues to expand and leave the massive recession of 2008/2009 behind, there will be a strong need for an increased number of technology jobs. For the U.S. GDP to continue to grow and provide good jobs of all types throughout the economy, it will need to turn more to India to solve its technology needs.

India is a diverse culture forged from a violent history of being conquered by various groups that impacted how it evolved to an offshoring powerhouse. After 1,000 AD, northern India was invaded and ultimately ruled by Muslim Asian nomads. While clearly of a different culture than the Hindu Indians, the new rulers mostly left the native population to their own customs and beliefs. Muslim rule lasted approximately until the 18th century when it started to disintegrate. A lasting effect of their long rule was a blending of cultures.

Today, roughly 20% of the population of India is Muslim, and many Indian laws are written for Islamic culture. Most of the revered Indian historical sites are monuments to Muslims such as the Taj Mahal. It was built as a tomb for the favorite wife of Mughal emperor Shah Jahan. The Taj Majal is one of the few world attractions more amazing than its pictures.

About the time that the Muslim rule was disintegrating in the north of India, Great Britain started to colonize it, starting with coastal outposts set up by the East India Company (also known as the Company) in the early 18th century. The Company slowly usurped power throughout India by force or by creating alliances with Indian princes. Those that allied with the Company were treated with respect and honor by the British, and they were left to directly administer the lands that ruled. By the 1820s, the Company had fully seized all of India.

During its rule until 1947, the East India Company had two long lasting effects on India. They imported the British justice system and set up a strong education system that was based on the English language. Some of the leaders of the Company were very religious and wanted to export their culture to India, but later leaders found the usefulness of educating natives in English for the Company's growing bureaucracy. During its rule, the Company roughly doubled the literacy rate.

Today, India has an extensive and internationally competitive university system, third largest in the world behind China and the United States. It will likely overtake the U.S. in the next decade with the overall number of its university graduates. More importantly, India currently graduates the largest number of Technology graduates than any other nation.

Visiting India

I had an opportunity to visit India as part of my job, and it was an incredible experience. The trip was a mix of sightseeing and work, so I was able to get a new perspective of the nation from many angles. My first shocking cultural sight after I landed at the airport was that most of the signs (street and business) in the major cities were in English. While I was aware that English was a strong second language in India, I didn't know how prevalent it was. I soon discovered that English is more than just a second language; it is the first language of Indian business.

Contracts in India are always written in English. In technology offices throughout India, emails between two Indians are always written in English. Many private schools require that only English is allowed to be spoken. The most unusual testament to this diversity of language can be found during casual conversation between Indians that are conversing in Hindi. English sentences and phrases are consistently mixed into these conversations.

Most Americans that work with Indians in an offshore engagement believe that their Indian counterpart struggles with understanding the language. It is pretty clear that Indians' command of

English in email form is excellent, but it comes across differently in conversation. Cultural differences contribute more to communication issues than comprehension of English. When visiting in person, there was a better comfort level of the Indian staff to be more vocal and opinionated than they were on conference calls. Also, I met a large number of very impressive technical resources that were on par with the big U.S. consulting firms. Clearly, they had leadership qualities that I had not realized nor taken advantage of.

For a country that was occupied for roughly 850 years, it is amazing that India has blended some of the cultures from its conquerors into its own. Instead of rejecting them, it venerates its Muslim historical sites and made English a reflection of the higher classes. Combined with its strong education system, India's strength in English has become the backbone for its huge technology sector.

One of the shocking parts of my visit to India was the paradox between the obvious wealth and scarcity that can be seen throughout many of the urban centers. Booming construction is everywhere you turn, and the number of people living in hardship is also obvious. One bedroom condos in Mumbai can cost the same as New York, but Mumbai is also the location of the largest slum in the world. There are huge numbers of modern office housing complexes throughout the nation as nice as anywhere in the world. However, the sheer size of the population

13 – The Politics of Offshoring

remains an overwhelming burden on the social services of the Indian government.

My view of India had changed at the conclusion of my trip. Indians had a much better command of the English language than I thought. Their technical resources and leadership skills were incredibly impressive, and their office was nicer than where I worked each day. I realized that the teams that I worked with in India were my peers in every aspect of technology.

Get Back in Front

14 – One Team Offshoring

14

ONE TEAM OFFSHORING

My company didn't have an engagement with an offshore consulting company, but they decided that they wanted to move in that direction aggressively. It is a lengthy process to get started. Selecting the right consulting company to have a long term engagement with takes a lot of evaluation and estimation. Negotiating the contract and labor rates is very complicated. The infrastructure has to be set up so that offshore resources have secure access to the company's network, and the network security of their computers in India has to have special requirements. In addition, the building security at offshore work locations needs to be agreed to.

One of the largest consulting companies in India was selected as our primary offshore vendor, and the contract was finalized. Since infrastructure improvements would take some time to create, it was decided that the first interaction between the two companies would be lower cost developers sent over from India to the U.S. for three year engagements. I was assigned one of the first five developers.

The number of resources that want to come to the U.S. for a three to six year assignment is very high within Indian consulting companies so their enthusiasm for the assignment is always excellent. The resource assigned to me was not trained in the applications that I worked on, but he was very motivated and resourceful. He was also extremely polite and hardworking. He quickly became an important member of my development team, and I was very impressed. His consulting rate in the U.S. was much cheaper than a typical U.S. consulting resource of equal skill level.

A year later, the bank completed the infrastructure needed to implement full offshoring. The initial engagements were mostly production support or very small staff augmentation assignments, and both organizations were looking for a large project to expand the operation. At the same time, I had started a project to create a big data mart and needed a large team of data transformation developers. I volunteered my project to be the guinea pig. It was going to be a good test of the vendor's ability to complete large development work offshore and in a technical space that had huge continuous demand. Designing and testing would still be conducted onshore in the U.S.

The standard staffing model of international offshoring consulting companies is to have one or

14 – One Team Offshoring

more consultants located on-site to be the primary interface with the offshore team. The on-site consultant's primary responsibility is to sit next to and work directly with the customers in order to work on design documents and communicate with the offshore teams. They are the conduit for issue resolution, and they ensure that both sides are on the same page. The consulting company usually selects the on-site and offshore resources while providing resumes to their clients.

That model is the primary reason why offshoring has a bad reputation around the world. What usually happens next is that offshore teams take requirements and then designs and code a solution. They ask questions through their on-site resource, and meetings will occur with clients to resolve issues. At the completion of development and system testing, they deliver a solution to the clients for testing, and it is almost always a disappointment. Clients find that they saved a lot of money but got exactly what they paid for. The final solution almost always has a number of issues that take longer to fix than the project plan allowed.

Going into this data warehousing project, I wanted to avoid finding big requirements gaps after receiving major components of the code from the offshore team. I decided that I was going to project manage the offshore team directly. My team and I were going to interview and select all the candidates for leadership roles in the offshore team. Clearly, there were better candidates than others, and good staffing decisions would really impact the success of the engagement.

The standard model is for an offshore project manager to create a project plan and deliver updates on progress. However, I insisted that my team and I have co-responsibility for estimates for the offshore developers in the plan. I agreed for an offshore project manager be part of the leadership of the overall team, and we mutually agreed that estimating would be worked on by both teams.

My next decision was the most important decision I would make in the evolution my offshore engagement model. I decided to forego the on-site coordinator and instead rely on a one team approach with direct communication between my team leads and the offshore leadership team. Even if the on-site coordinator did a great job, it was still a level of worthless bureaucracy that I felt could be eliminated. The new communication hurdles could be eliminated with effort and time.

The first obstacle was finding the right time of day that both teams would interact. With a 10.5 hour time zone difference between Eastern Standard Time and India Standard Time, both groups would completely miss each other if everyone worked the first shift. Sending emails back and forth that could take 24 hours to respond to was not acceptable. Fortunately, Indian consulting teams are used to having a very strong second shift, and it is an easy work shift for them to staff. The third shift in Indian time is very

14 – One Team Offshoring

hard to staff. My decision on a second shift team created 3 hours a day where both teams would be in the office at the same time and could meet, email, or message each other.

The second obstacle was ensuring an adequate dialogue between the two teams. That was solved by creating a daily half hour call where attendance by leaders from both sides was required. While it appeared to be a heavy burden on everyone's calendar, it was absolutely necessary for a number of reasons. It ensured that the combined team discussed every issue every day. Team members were able to get comfortable with each other's personalities, and camaraderie and humor evolved as a result. When they became comfortable with each other, it increased communication in emails and messaging. If the call needed to extend between a smaller group, everyone else would drop off when the topics narrowed.

As time went on, the team continued to grow closer. Some people on both continents became Facebook friends. Pictures were exchanged and hung in each teams' offices so that we were reminded what face went to what name. If someone was out with a sick child, the whole team knew about it. When there were holidays, each side understood what the holiday was all about.

It seemed too simple. It seemed too easy. A short daily call of all project team leaders was the secret to resolving almost every issue and complaint that people have about offshoring.

The daily call shortened the distance between us, and it took out the cultural issues. It took out language issues. It removed every obstacle we had. Instead of thinking that our Indian peers were on the other side of the world, it seemed as if they were on the other side of the building. When you move past that psychological hurdle, you realize that there really isn't onshore or offshore or consulting company. There is just ONE team.

The project was a big success. It finished on time, within budget, with quality, and offshoring cut the project costs in half. Senior Management was impressed, and I received a lot of positive exposure. It also encouraged me to take the next step.

Evolution

The next big project was twice as large but had similar objectives to create a large data mart. It would require twice as many developers as the other project, but I was able to keep my offshore team intact. Since the original offshore engagement went so well, I decided to expand the scope of the offshore team to add detailed design and system testing to their project goals. The offshore team had to add data modelers, data analysts, testing resources, and the combined team size grew to roughly 100.

There was a side benefit that I had not expected. When you start interviewing and adding a larger number of offshore leaders to your team, you start increasing the odds that you will find resources that are truly brilliant and can evolve into the critical design resources for the combined onshore and offshore team. In the second data mart project I found those people.

Becoming an information technology professional in the United States is very different than in India. In the U.S., there are many different paths that people can evolve into the profession. One path is to migrate to a technical position within a company from a non-technical role. There are many people that start as clients that decide they want to move over into technology units. Another path is through school training. Americans can choose to major in computer science or management information systems in a college or university. Or, there are plenty of two year technical schools or junior colleges that are easy to get accepted to.

In India, there are a billion people, and technology positions are more popular there than in the United States. Getting accepted into computer science programs in Indian universities is highly competitive and selective. In the U.S., you can just choose computer science as a major, but in India, it is a major achievement to get into that career field.

Does that mean that Indian developers are better on average than their U.S. counterparts? Indian developers are proven to be more academically competitive, but American project managers find U.S. developers' soft skills such as project management capabilities to be a great equalizer. However, the highly competitive nature of the Indian technology industry dramatically increases the odds that you can find brilliant technical leaders for a fraction of the cost of hiring a similarly talented person in the U.S.

The very best technology developers and architects in the U.S. generally work in Silicon Valley or for consulting companies where the pay can be roughly double that of an average U.S. company. Consulting rates for these individuals end up being incredibly high and outside the budget of many projects. If you bring in a team from IBM, you will get some of the best, but you will pay for it too.

When you engage a team from India, you can search for and find senior developers that easily rival the best that Silicon Valley and consulting companies have to offer for a price that is one-tenth of the cost. If you need three of these top caliber technical leads, you can find them. Some will even emerge over time from the ranks of the lower experienced group working for your team. If you are having a hard time finding a great resource or two, you can push the Indian consulting company to reassign some of their brighter stars to your project. They will accommodate assertive clients.

The results from the second data mart project were excellent. Again, it delivered on time and within budget with quality. The difference is that it saved the company $3 million and showed that a huge offshore team with full project responsibilities could deliver as well or better than an internal team. Having the designers sitting close by the developers and testers really paid off. By the time the project completed, we had identified at least three technical leaders that were as good as anyone I had ever worked with.

Next Big Step

There was another large project that took this offshore model to an even higher level. My next assignment was completely different than the first two. It was not another data warehousing effort which is a technical space that offshore companies already have large skilled staffs with high competency. I had to build a web based application to run a huge department in the bank. The offshore team that I had been working with was disbanded, and a new one had to be built. The new application was going to be a complete custom build, so it was going to be much more challenging than the other projects.

I interviewed a number of offshore resources for leadership roles. Priority was placed on those that had a diverse set of experiences in various tools because the new application was going to use a lot of different software tools. I settled on two developers for my technical leads. They had already led a few projects on web based applications with success, and they interviewed extremely well. They turned out to be more than I had hoped for.

The offshore technical leads were so clearly

competent that they were immediately included in the architectural process and became leaders in the design phase. As the offshore staff ramped up, they helped interview and select every candidate and led the training efforts to get everyone up to speed. All code designs were managed by them, and they oversaw the development of use cases for testing.

That project finished as a big success. It completed my third successive large offshore engagement in the bank and really received the attention of senior management. I was known around the company as someone that could make offshoring work, and I started getting invited to speak about it to other groups. My consistent message was that there is enormous opportunity to be found in India, and you can easily find it with just a few simple process changes.

There are very few managers or project managers in the U.S. that are viewed within their company as being successful at offshoring. Instead of putting in the extra effort to excel at it, they spend more time trying to figure out excuses as to why it is the consulting company's fault. Offshoring is a great and surprisingly easy opportunity to create a unique image as a resource that can out achieve your peers.

14 – One Team Offshoring

> Rule 37: Manage the project yourself instead of relying on offshore project managers to manage it
>
> Rule 38: Interview and select key offshore resources yourself
>
> Rule 39: Create a daily conference call between both onshore and offshore teams
>
> Rule 40: Get to know the offshore resources personally as if they sat next to you

Get Back in Front

15

MANAGING REMOTE STAFF

The number of technology professionals telecommuting or working from their home office is growing every day. The obvious benefit to employees is no transportation cost or time spent commuting. The quality of life impact could be 10 or more extra hours a week spent with family or friends.

Most companies are now also aware of the tremendous benefits associated with remote staff for them as well.

1. There are huge cost savings in facilities charges of thousands of dollars a year per resource.

2. It increases business resiliency in the event of a facilities disaster.

3. Companies are often constrained by the labor pool in their footprint and now they can go outside of that to recruit nationally.

4. Turnover is naturally lower with employees that work out of their home.

5. Even if they believe that they can make more money switching to a new company, resources are less likely to take on additional commuting time and costs.

While a remote staffing workplace seems like a great idea, it also presents a productivity risk to companies. Managers are far away from their staff so supervision can be a challenge, and interaction with co-workers is usually reduced. The best way to overcome that is to have a corporate or personnel strategy that sets clear standards for managing remote staff.

There are two types of remote staff, those that transfer into that role and those that are hired into it. If someone is not a great resource to begin with, it is unlikely their manager would approve their working from home. Low productivity will only become lower. Great resources are self-motivated and highly accountable, and their transfer to a remote model usually has no impact on their productivity. Resources that are hired into a new role and start in the remote model have to be monitored more closely for a period of time. Most companies have a 60 to 90 day grace period where a new employee can be terminated by their hiring manager without a complex HR review. New remote resources need to prove that they can be very productive in that model quickly, or they should be let go.

15 – Managing Remote Staff

The best tool for managing remote staff is a messaging tool. Most messaging tools have the ability to tell the general status of a user. It will show whether someone logged into their workstations to start their day or logged out to end their day. When the workstation goes into sleep mode, the user's status will reflect logged in but not currently available. The ability to track the remote resource's availability is very important for a manager to judge if the resource is working their normal assigned workday. The messaging service also makes communication much easier between a remote resource and others because it makes it clear that the person is ready to respond immediately to any question or comment. Emails typically have a protocol for a response by the end of the day or within 24 hours, but instant messages require a near immediate response.

Another critical tool for a manager is a twice weekly conference call. If there are multiple remote employees on a single team, a short half hour informal call with the entire team is a great way to ensure that remote resources are keeping productive and interactive with others. Proximity in the office creates a lot of incidental communication that is lost when a resource works from their home, and it needs to be replicated via the phone. The forced interaction is important even with a light agenda at each meeting.

The de-motivating aspect of remote work can't be ignored, and a manager has to modify their approach. Home has a million distractions that the work place doesn't, such as other family members, pets, kids, and chores. Not everyone can succeed at working from home. The manager has to be aware of this risk and spend more time micromanaging the remote resource until that person proves that they are succeeding. Normally, managers have to spend 80% of their time managing the weakest 20% of their staff. While a new remote resource is too new to be rated weak, the approach should be similar. They need to be managed and watched as if they are a poor performer until they prove that they can consistently produce.

It's beneficial for managers to set clear standards and routines for their own interaction with remote staff. Managers can quickly forget about resources that they don't see every day. The more time a manager invests early in a new remote work assignment, the sooner they can reduce interaction after they have learned its strengths and weaknesses.

Time zone issues are also important. Team members on an opposite coast have to compensate by at least two hours to work a shift that is routine for the primary company time zone. If they work outside that routine time zone, it reduces their availability to other team members and their ability to be productive.

If the corporate budget allows, have team members come to the office two or three times a year. Have the team go to dinner together and bond outside the work environment. Those little trips can have a lasting impact on people's comfort levels for communicating with each other.

15 – Managing Remote Staff

Managers that create a successful image as thriving with remote staff create opportunities for themselves. Senior management will usually look to those that can adapt to a broad geographic resource pool for added responsibilities and promotions.

> Rule 41: Micromanage new remote employees for a period of time until they prove they can be productive
>
> Rule 42: Use instant messaging tools and conference calls as critical tools to manage remote resources
>
> Rule 43: Bring the team together physically as often as the corporate budget will allow

Get Back in Front

16

FASTER CAREER ADVANCEMENT

All of the rules in this book are designed to improve your image with your target audience within your company for raises and promotion opportunities. However, there is a clear faster alternative to advancing your career. An impressive resume, good interviewing skills, and the ability to move anywhere in the United States will take you farther faster.

Every medium to large corporation in the U.S. has fairly strict guidelines on how much money is available across the corporation for reviews and promotions. If it has a 3% increase limit in overall salaries annually, all promotions and raises have to fit within that guideline. When managers factor promotions into their budget, the end result is usually a raise of 5% for those with a superior rating. Promotions also tend to be limited to less than a 10% increase.

That may sound like a very nice percentage increase unless you are grossly underpaid. People that regularly outperform their peers and take on responsibilities higher than their pay grade will stay poorly paid compared to the marketplace. Even with a promotion, staying with one company will leave them underpaid.

For example, consider a scenario where a junior project manager starts out with a salary of $55,000 and gets above average ratings for four years. After the fourth year, that person is promoted to mid-level project manager. When you factor 4.5% increases for 3 years and a 10% promotion the fourth year, that $55,000 becomes $69,000. That would be a stellar four years of work and ratings. At the same time, the market for moderately experienced project managers is likely $80,000 (depending on market) for someone with the same skill level at that same company. Unfortunately, most companies are not allowed by HR guidelines to just promote this resource into an $80,000 position. At the same time the four year high achiever gets promoted, their company is likely hiring external resources into that same role at $80,000.

It seems horribly unfair and it is. If you like your company and locale, then you have a tough decision to make. You can keep working to move up the ladder in the same company for less pay, or you can take the path of dramatically more money and responsibility. You can plan your career to aggressively move up by changing companies and jobs.

The benefits of moving to different companies in different cities extends beyond pay and position title.

16 – Faster Career Advancement

It helps to add new experiences and skills with new technologies to your resume. It might even add a new type of business to your resume. As long as you stay three years with a company, the next company that interviews you won't perceive you as a pure mercenary. Three different companies in ten years with a variety of experiences look very good on a resume. Conversely, you might get stuck doing the same types of projects in the same company for a long time. Each experience has a shelf life on its appeal to potential employers before they start to question why you didn't move on to something bigger or better.

The cost of moving around the country is pretty steep as well. Friends and family become a vacation stop instead of a daily part of your life. Just when you make friends in your new company or neighborhood, you will be packing up and moving on. If you are married with children, it becomes a hardship for your spouse and children as well.

Geography is a big part of moving up. Everyone may want to live in Manhattan or Malibu, but Fargo and Birmingham may have the best jobs available. Less prime locations usually have less people willing to move there so they often offer better pay and benefits. If moving up quickly is the primary goal, then geography has to be initially ruled out as a deciding factor. Later in your career, you will have the option to move to better geography as your resume develops.

When companies advertise open positions for project managers or managers, the requirements are almost always the same regardless of experience level. Similar to managers, junior project managers have to manage budget, staffing and clients. The degree of responsibility is larger and requires more polish and skills, but moving up to a more challenging role is the right ambition for a motivated person.

My Experience

During the early years in my career, I moved to different geographic locations and positions in some of the largest companies in the financial services industry. My resume assembled some very impressive names and titles on it, and my level of responsibility increased significantly each time. When I reached my early 30s, children and stability became more of a priority, and I decided to stay within one company and climb the ladder there.

Moving from new college graduate to senior project manager was completed in less than 10 years, but it slowed down after that. The number of competent people competing at that level was quite high, and the next promotion appeared to be a long way off. Then I had the training session that I outlined on page one and everything changed for me. I developed these rules that aided in my development, and I was promoted two levels in fairly quick order. You can too.

16 – Faster Career Advancement

Rule 44: Stay in one position for at least three years

Rule 45: Rule out geography if moving up quicker is the priority

Get Back in Front

Appendix

APPENDIX

Rule 1 (Chapter 1): Spend more time and energy improving your image than improving your performance

Rule 2 (Chapter 2): Start your work day at 7:55 am and end it at 5:05 pm.

Rule 3 (Chapter 2): Respond instantly to anything from your target audience, even if you have to stop something else to do so

Rule 4 (Chapter 2): Slowly and thoroughly review the accuracy of every word in your reply before you respond

Rule 5 (Chapter 3): Place yourself in places or opportunities that force you to get energized

Rule 6 (Chapter 3): Reflect an image of a high energy person that's passionate about your job

Rule 7 (Chapter 3): Set 10 or 20 year goals, and rate your progress every New Year

Rule 8 (Chapter 4):   If you are not sure what direction to go, choose the best option and get traction towards it immediately

Rule 9 (Chapter 4):   Advertise successes to your target audience regularly

Rule 10 (Chapter 4):   Identify higher risk tasks and get traction on those immediately and every day

Rule 11 (Chapter 4):   When trying to motivate someone, be nice, sensitive, and unrelenting

Rule 12 (Chapter 5):   Become an expert at knowing who can do what in your company's bureaucracy

Rule 13 (Chapter 6):   Be consistent in your approach to everything so that management and team resources know what to expect from you every time

Rule 14 (Chapter 6):   Set high expectations and goals for the team and individuals

Rule 15 (Chapter 6):   Assign weak resources only one task at a time to maximize their value

Rule 16 (Chapter 6):   Be very loyal so that others will go the extra mile for you

Rule 17 (Chapter 7):   Get as many resources as possible to attend a conference call without giving full disclosure of the details of the fire drill

Rule 18 (Chapter 7):   Keep the conference call going as long as it takes to resolve your file drill

Appendix

Rule 19 (Chapter 7): Don't believe when people say "no" so ask 5 times in different ways

Rule 20 (Chapter 8): Make all meetings an advertisement for how skilled and smart you are

Rule 21 (Chapter 8): If you have to present a topic to your target audience, over prepare for it

Rule 22 (Chapter 9): Never underestimate your inability to estimate correctly

Rule 23 (Chapter 9): Never underestimate anyone else's inability to estimate correctly

Rule 24 (Chapter 9): Use offshore for as much project work as possible to protect your estimates

Rule 25 (Chapter 9): Use your top down estimate as the primary estimate and your bottom up estimate as validation

Rule 26 (Chapter 9): Be the first to anchor any project timeline or budget

Rule 27 (Chapter 10): Make sure your requirements document is as complete as possible because missing requirements will destroy a project

Rule 28 (Chapter 10): Never add requirements that the client isn't asking for

Rule 29 (Chapter 10): Ensure that "nice to have" items are never included in a requirements document

Rule 30 (Chapter 10): Communicate to every

member of your team that they will be held accountable to the requirements document so they need to meaningfully participate in the process

Rule 31 (Chapter 10):   Avoid at all costs any assignment requesting you to save a project

Rule 32 (Chapter 11):   Use Gantt Charts to communicate your project plan to your target audience

Rule 33 (Chapter 11):   Do not get bogged down spending too much time managing too many tasks in your project plan

Rule 34 (Chapter 11):   Avoid frivolous data in your project plan because it will take time away from effective leadership

Rule 35 (Chapter 12):   At the onset of any project, make sure that everyone knows that they have two jobs: project manager and their official assignment

Rule 36 (Chapter 12):   Find and dedicate at least 10 minutes every day to market your image

Rule 37 (Chapter 14):   Manage the project yourself instead of relying on offshore project managers to manage it

Rule 38 (Chapter 14):   Interview and select key offshore resources yourself

Rule 39 (Chapter 14):   Create a daily conference call between both onshore and offshore teams

Appendix

Rule 40 (Chapter 14): Get to know the offshore resources personally as if they sat next to you

Rule 41 (Chapter 15): Micromanage new remote employees for a period of time until they prove they can be productive

Rule 42 (Chapter 15): Use instant messaging tools and conference calls as critical tools to manage remote resources

Rule 43 (Chapter 15): Bring the team together physically as often as the corporate budget will allow

Rule 44 (Chapter 16): Stay in one position for at least three years

Rule 45 (Chapter 16): Rule out geography if moving up quicker is the priority

Get Back in Front

ABOUT THE AUTHOR

Brad Cormier is currently a Vice President in Information Technology in a top ten U.S. bank. Without a prestigious degree or connections, he had to navigate his career from the bottom up. He successfully discovered the tools and techniques to master the politics of the business office environment. He has managed $20 million projects and hundreds of employees that executed these same rules for amazing results. **He resides in the greater Cleveland area with his wife and six children.**

www.ingramcontent.com/pod-product-compliance
Lightning Source LLC
Chambersburg PA
CBHW051702170526
45167CB00002B/508